GREAT

~~ANSWERS~~

to Tough

MARKETING

QUESTIONS

GREAT
Answers
to Tough
MARKETING
QUESTIONS

P R Smith

**KOGAN
PAGE**

First published 1999

Kogan Page Limited
120 Pentonville Road
London
N1 9JN
UK

Kogan Page Limited
163 Central Avenue, Suite 4
Dover
NH 03820
USA

British Library Cataloguing in Publication Data

A CIP record for this book is available from the British Library.

ISBN 0 7494 3018 4

Typeset by Jo Brereton, Primary Focus, Haslington, Cheshire
Printed and bound in Great Britain by Bell & Bain Ltd, Glasgow

contents

foreword
by Warren Keegan

Best-selling author, Paul Smith, has done it again. This book should have been written years ago as it takes the mystery out of marketing, while its easy-to-digest approach makes marketing available to anyone who has an interest in meeting needs and creating value.

This book is both refreshing and different. It provides quick access to the world of marketing in a light, easy and entertaining way. The succinct nature of the writing combined with the often humorous approach allows readers to 'dip in' and extract meaningful answers to popular questions.

This book presents simple, sensible answers to the marketing questions you have, or that you should have, in a punchy and entertaining way. It makes marketing accessible to all – those new to marketing, those who wonder what 'the marketing people actually do for a living' and those more experienced marketers who want to avoid bad habits and brush up on marketing concepts and tools.

If you are interested in taking advantage of the power of the marketing discipline to realize greater success in your business or organization, buy this book. You can put it on your shelf for reference, or read it from cover to cover: in either case you will be richly rewarded for your effort with greater market and competitive success.

Dr Warren Keegan
Professor of Marketing and International Business and Director of the Institute for Global Business Strategy at the Lubin School of Business, Pace University, New York

preface
— how to use this book

This book contains the answers to many burning questions about marketing. It is written in a light, easy-to-read and entertaining manner. Each question is succinctly answered and supported by an intriguing visual or a thought-provoking quote, to create a friendly, pleasant and easily digestible book on marketing.

The questions are grouped into typical, topical areas as follows:

- Marketing
- Segmentation, Positioning and the Marketing Mix
- Planning
- Buyer Behaviour
- Marketing Research
- Products
- Services
- Pricing
- Distribution
- Integrated Marketing Communications

So if you have a question about marketing check the contents pages (which list all the questions under each of the above groupings) to see if the question or similar question is listed. Then read the answer. Alternatively, you can peruse the questions and see if you can answer them. If you can't answer the question, read the answer. Then ask yourself the question a week later and see if you can remember the answer. If you cannot, read it again. If you have a question that is not listed perhaps you might be kind enough to send it to me (c/o Kogan Page) and I will endeavour to include it in future editions.

If you find yourself particularly interested in a specific area or answer and would like to explore the area in greater depth, then you will find the copious references to the Marketing CD ROMs (see pages 275–76) and one or two other sources listed at the end of each section. In fact, most of the answers are drawn from the basic tutorial text that I originally wrote for the Marketing CD ROM series. The references point you towards additional video interviews with world gurus (Peter Doyle, Philip Kotler and Theodore Levitt, Rosabeth Moss Kanter and Kenichi Ohmae) and top marketing directors from major blue chip companies (from Microsoft to Manchester United and Coca-Cola to Concorde).

We live in changing times. I hope you enjoy this new format for a book and I welcome any comments, criticisms, suggestions and improvements that you might care to send me.

Best wishes

Paul Smith

acknowledgements

My thanks to:

Chris Berry   Alan Munro
Peter Betts   Alan Pulford
Pauline Goodwin   Dennis Sandler
Warren Keegan   Steven Saunders
Hugh Lacey   Shane Smith
Martin Lello

and the world gurus who kindly gave me the interviews for the Marketing CD ROMs and whose thoughts (and their other publications) have subsequently influenced my writing:

Peter Doyle   Rosabeth Moss Kanter
Philip Kotler   Kenichi Ohmae
Theodore Levitt

and the top marketing directors who also kindly gave me the opportunity to interview them (for the Marketing CD ROM series) and examine how the best companies really succeed in marketing:

George Bradt, Coca-Cola   Peter Liney, Concorde/British Airways
Sam Howe, Southwestern Bell   Ken Merrett, Manchester United
John Leftwich, Microsoft

Thanks also to the whole Multimedia Marketing Consortium team:

Adeeba, Alan, Caspar, Chris, Imran, Kingsley, Kully, Mubarak, Peter and Ze.

Eternal thanks to Bev and our beanies, Aran, Cian and Lily, for being wonderful in more ways than they will ever know.

On top of all of this, thank you to the little man who waited patiently in the rain beside the post box.

Paul Smith

one

basic **concepts** **and definitions** **of marketing**

- When did it all start?
- Change, change, change. Do we really have to?
- Who needs marketing?
- Why are most companies weak at marketing?
- What is marketing?
- Is marketing an art or a science?
- Why bother with researching needs and wants?
- In marketing, is something always exchanged?
- What are lifetime values?
- Are markets becoming more competitive?

When did it all start?

Marketing is a relatively young discipline. Some, however, argue that it has been around for a long time.

Trade and payment in money, goods and services has been around for many thousands of years. Barter or counter trade is becoming popular in business again. Counter trade is more common than you think, for example, some chemical companies often accept non-monetary payment, such as other chemicals, as payment from their customers.

Some argue that marketing has been in existence whenever and wherever there have been buyers and sellers, ie, a market. Some marketing tools, such as advertising, have been around for hundreds and even thousands of years. The Ancient Greeks used advertising for commercial purposes. The traders hired 'criers' to promote their products. Their advertising propositions were sometimes surprisingly similar to today's television advertisements. But none of the ancient brands lasted the test of time. Few brands last a century let alone a millennium or two. A disciplined approach to marketing has only emerged towards the end of the second millennium and sadly was practised by only a handful of organizations.

There are, however, a few select brands which have been around for a few hundred years, for example, Guinness since 1759 and Pears since 1789. There were many famous brands created during the 19th century. Some have survived. But in reality few brands succeed in the long term. Fewer still survive two centuries of change. The great marketing graveyard in the sky is littered with once famous brands that were regularly bought by legions of 'loyal' customers. Where are they now? Why have they gone? What caused their demise? Why do you think these once famous and successful brands eventually failed?

There are many underlying change factors in the macro-environment such as fashion and technology which, if ignored, can affect a market or even kill off a brand. Everything changes – including lifestyles, values and attitudes. Some of yesterday's products and their advertisements may seem strange today, but they were considered normal in their own time. Do you think that society reflects advertising or advertising reflects society?

Advertisements can give an insight particularly into how fashions, values and attitudes change. Whichever way you look at it 'change' affects markets. So serious marketers constantly monitor any changes and move with the market. Those that don't get left behind and join the great marketing graveyard in the sky.

Few brands survive the test of time

Change, change, change. Do we really have to?

Change has been constant throughout the history of marketing. Markets are in a constant state of change. To survive, you have to move with the market. To do this, you have to change your marketing.

The only certainty is change. Everything changes – customers grow old, develop new tastes, acquire new values, earn different amounts, and prioritize 'new' needs while new competitors emerge, laws and regulations change and technology sends out shock waves. Nothing stays the same. The world and marketing are changing. They will continue to change.

Today's winners may be tomorrow's losers. It has been said that 'success is the temporary suspension of failure'. Guess what percentage of the world's 500 most successful companies (Fortune 500) in 1957 still exist today? Thirty-three per cent or one-third of the companies who were at the top of the business league table in 1957 still survive today. Success is momentary. There is no time to rest on one's laurels. More recently, the best selling business book in the 80s, *In Search Of Excellence*, highlighted 46 out-standingly excellent companies. How many of these so-called excellent companies of the 80s have survived today? Answer: 6.

Continual success requires continual monitoring and responses to change – often before the change actually occurs. The rate of change accelerated when television burst onto the scene in the 1950s. Today's computers, satellite, cable, multimedia, and virtual reality networks and the Internet are also changing markets, and they change way we buy, the way we sell, the products and services we want, and the way we communicate, receive and even pay for tomorrow's brands. Change is rampant. Witness Tokyo's oxygen bars and the emergence of thought-operated computers. It's not long ago when Eurovision song contest winners dressed in dresses were women and families had two parents. Once upon a time Germany was split in two, communism controlled chunks of Europe and China kept her doors firmly shut to the West. That's all changed now. Today's borderless world has new power bases, with more than half (51 per cent) of the world's largest economic groupings emerging as companies, while only 49 per cent are countries.

So marketers keep their antennae out, observe change and respond to it. They look towards long-term changes and future market trends that may affect, directly or indirectly, their markets. Today's marketers have to be keen observers of change. We all are surrounded by change. Back in AD 500, Heraclitus, the Greek philosopher, spotted it too, 'You cannot step twice into the same river for fresh waters are ever flowing in upon you.'

Change creeps up slowly and takes over while leaving many behind

or

> **❝**If the rate of change inside a company is less than the rate of change outside a company, then the end is in sight.**❞**
>
> *Jack Welch, EX CEO, General Electric*

Who needs marketing?

Since the 1970s there has been a rapid adoption of some marketing techniques across a wide variety of organizations. It's not just big corporations that use marketing techniques. Perhaps once it would have been vilified by churches, but today many different types of organizations, including many churches, see marketing as crucial to their survival.

From police to political parties, charities to churches, ballet to boxing most organizations use marketing techniques to a certain degree. Today even public institutions, such as the Inland Revenue, are becoming interested in marketing. Everyone needs marketing.

Although a wide variety of organizations use some marketing techniques, this does not mean that they are truly marketing orientated. Even profit-making corporations fall into bad habits and allow their marketing efforts to drift away from real marketing orientation by not constantly looking and listening to the marketplace and striving to improve beyond the competition and competitive benchmarks. In addition to continual improvement in customer care, customer retention and product design, today's marketing requires constant research into changing customers, competition, communications, distribution channels, product development, pricing, etc.

Everyone needs marketing. There appears to be a widespread adoption of marketing techniques, such as advertising and mail shots. This is not, however, the same as widespread adoption of a proper, disciplined approach to marketing that stays close to the customer, collects feedback and develops new and improved products for tomorrow. So although every organization needs marketing, there is, in reality, a sad lack of real marketing excellence out there.

Every organization needs marketing

Why are most companies weak at marketing?

Although there is widespread use of marketing techniques, only a few organizations are actually truly marketing orientated. They do not constantly research their markets, including their competitors as well as their customers... they do not continually seek improvements in customer care and product quality, and they do not embrace change wholeheartedly. They also forget to address the fundamentals. Consider this recent list of examples of pathetic marketing:

- 90 per cent of British companies don't know their customers.[1]
- 50 per cent of UK Web marketing consultancies had flawed Web sites.[2]
- 50 per cent of major German companies failed to reply to an e-mail enquiry within four days.[3]
- 49 per cent of British companies could not identify customers at risk of defection.[4]
- 43 per cent of British companies were unable to identify why they lose customers.[5]

There appears to be a high level of marketing awareness, but not a corresponding level of proper application. The UK's Chartered Institute of Marketing (CIM) once said that, 'We have the knowledge but not the enthusiasm.' CIM also pointed out that a majority of British companies do not engage in real marketing since they do not carry out any market research. Can you guess what percentage of British companies did not carry out market research during the height of marketing awareness in the 80s? A staggering 66 per cent. Two-thirds did not bother to do any market research. This suggests that there has been a lack of truly marketing orientated organizations in Britain alone. Has it improved? Look around you and see. In 1999, research revealed 50 per cent do not carry out regular usage and attitude surveys; 44 per cent said the customer is rarely, if ever, represented round the boardroom table; 57 per cent of companies with over £1 billion turnover had no board level marketing director.[6]

How many organizations do you think are excellent at their marketing?

What is marketing?

Writing definitions is not easy. There are many different definitions of marketing. Some are better than others.

Marketing can be defined as a range of activities including advertising, selling, PR, sales promotion, direct mail, pricing, market research, and so on. It can, arguably, be better defined as a philosophy or approach to business. Various marketing bodies from around the world have different definitions. Here is the UK Chartered Institute of Marketing's definition: 'The management process responsible for identifying, anticipating and satisfying customer requirements profitably. The word profit, if taken literally, excludes the vast armies of not-for-profit organizations such as charities who have ultimate goals other than profit.'

Here are some marketing professionals defining marketing:

'The great thing about marketing is that it takes an hour to learn and a lifetime to master. I think that in itself it is one of the great bits of appeal about marketing. Drucker, the great management theorist had an equally appealing phrase which said that "The role of marketing is to make the sales force redundant". Sort of an aggressive approach, one which I like using with the sales force. Is he right or is he wrong? The truth of the matter is that if you take a classical definition of marketing... getting the right products in the right place at the right price at the right level of promotion. If you, as a marketer, do all those things then you can actually obviate the need for a sales force.' John Leftwich, European Marketing Director, Microsoft.

'In terms of defining marketing, I always find it is this sort of perennial question. My basic advise to anyone is to go and look in Kotler because that is where the answer is and he will tell all about the 4Ps (see page 36). And from a classic text book sense, I think that is what I would go for. From a sort of "What do I do on an operational day-to-day basis?", marketing is about identifying consumer needs, meeting those needs in terms of product dev-elopment and very effectively communicating to customers that you have met their needs and that includes pricing, that includes the right communication channels, it includes the right messages and the right media for those messages. One thing it is not is complex. Marketing is common sense applied.' Peter Liney, Marketing Manager, Concorde Supersonic Jet.

'I define marketing in a classic sense. It's about looking at people's needs and wants and matching them with certain products that are available now, today, or in the future.' Sam Howe, Marketing VP, SouthWestern Bell.

> **"Marketing is selling goods that don't come back to people that do."**
>
> *(source unknown)*

> **"Marketing is about being best at something important to your customers."**
>
> *(source unknown)*

Is marketing an art or a science?

Do you think marketing is an art or a science, or both?

Can marketing managers predict what will happen when they mix marketing ingredients together? If they reduce price will sales go up... or down?

Or if they increase advertising will sales go up... or down?... this week, this month, next year or in the long term... what will happen?

Are human beings conditioned by television advertising or by their neighbours, or are they totally free agents? Can scientific marketing managers play with aggregate numbers and deal with average changes across a wide universe? In the UK during the late 90s, 30 million people suddenly changed their behaviour patterns, shopping patterns and even leisure patterns at least once a week. Were they conditioned ruthlessly by a clever cocktail of advertising, PR and distribution when the UK's national lottery was launched? Did the marketing team predict these kind of responses?

Marketing moves beyond the realm of physical responses and into the realm of mental responses, such as shifts in awareness, attitudes, intentions to purchase, and so on. Can marketers 'buy share of mind', ie calculate how many advertisements it takes to achieve carefully determined levels of brand awareness? Marketers can predict the aggregate numbers of customers who will respond to direct mail shots or television advertisements. They can, therefore, mathematically calculate how many mail shots are required and how much money to spend to achieve specific objectives. They can also use sophisticated software packages to help to determine the optimum communications mix (advertising, PR, sales promotion, etc) and the optimum marketing mix (product features, price points, etc).

Or is there so much creativity in marketing that many would consider it to be an art form? So is it an art, a science, both or neither? What do you think?

Is marketing an art or a science?

Why bother with researching needs and wants?

Customers are at the centre of the marketing concept. Customer needs and wants are not always apparent. They have to be carefully and continually researched. There is, technically speaking, a difference between needs and wants. We have basic needs for food, shelter, love, and so on. Wants are specific desires. We all need food. Some people want a hamburger, others resent being offered a burger and prefer instead a vegetarian meal. Others again may prefer an Indian, Chinese or Mexican meal. The same person, in a different situation, might only want a plain bar of chocolate.

Understanding customers' needs and wants is absolutely vital for long-term survival. It can be difficult to keep abreast with changing customer requirements. Not everyone can spot a new product opportunity or a relevant market trend that satisfies a customer's, often hidden, needs. Even the best get it wrong, and misinterpret customer needs and wants. For example, Decca record company turned down the 1960s mega band, The Beatles, because they said 'groups with guitars are on their way out'. More recently, Coca-Cola misjudged the wants of the American people when they launched New Coke. It failed because they misunderstood how much people wanted (and loved) the old brand Coca-Cola more than a new and better tasting Coca-Cola.

Also, customer requirements change sometimes because of shifts in fashion, values, attitudes, lifestyle, disposable income or new technology becoming available. Who could have imagined that one day people would want to wear record players (Sony Walkmans) on their heads? Who could have imagined that society would one day condone this as normal behaviour?

It's not just customers who develop new requirements. Business and industrial organizations also develop new requirements. In the 1950s and 60s, businesses did not need computers to survive. By the 80s and 90s just about all organizations needed a computer. Who could imagine that one day organizations would also have a need for an information destroyer? Today the paper shredder is a common piece of office equipment. So the importance of certain needs and wants change. Constant research can reveal early indications of any changes that may appear on the horizon. This is the delicate job of marketing research.

There are different ways of looking at the same situation. There are different ways of using market research. The ability to ask the right questions is a skill. There are different types of questions that can be asked in order to assess the situation. Asking the right question reduces the risk of a costly mistake. There is one question that constantly needs to be asked: is there a need or does any one really want this product/service (at a particular price, from a particular store, promoted in a particular way)?

Collecting the right information is where skilled market research comes in. Research saves marketing managers from having to play guessing games. Research reduces risk. On the other hand, it also costs time, money and expertise. Customers, and the relative importance of their own needs, change all the time. Continual research is, therefore, required in order to continually understand changing customer needs and specific wants. Research, whether street surveys, small focus groups or simply customer conversations, lies at the heart good marketing.

> Knowing what question to ask is a great skill that requires practice.

In marketing, is something always exchanged?

Marketing, and the marketing concept, is dependent on exchange, for example, goods, services or benefits exchanged for cash or other services. Think about how this could apply to marketing a charity? What do donors get when they donate? What is exchanged? Money for what? An enlightened feeling, self-actualization, good feelings, peer acceptance, guilt relief? Why do people pay to go to football matches? What do they exchange... money for what in return? Marketers have to find answers to recurring questions such as what key benefits do customers want and get?

An exchange of mutual benefits where the customer receives utility, value and satisfaction, while the organization simultaneously achieves its own goals and objectives. For example, generating revenues or profits or, in the case of a non-profit-making organization, operating efficiently and effectively, which, in turn, allows it to survive and continue to fulfil its mission.

Underpinning all of this is common sense. You can increase the customer's benefits by adding value to the customer's experience by giving outstanding service. But you can only offer what is within your resources.

Take customer service. It can rise to ridiculously expensive levels. There may come a time when you cannot tend to every customer's whim because you simply do not have the staff to run back and forth.

This is the time to consider whether the extra service is appropriate.

- Is it really necessary or important to the customer (will you lose business if you withdraw this extra service)?
- Does the competition offer the same level of extra service?
- Can we afford it, or would customers be prepared to pay more for it?
- Is there a more cost-effective way of delivering the same service?

Most customer service costs very little. A smile can make all the difference. It is worth noting that the same staff can deliver either the best or worst customer service depending on their level of training and motivation. Research into what is required by customers and delivered by the competition helps to determine what really needs to be exchanged between the organization and its customers. 'Exchange' is an integral part of marketing.

Charities need to know what exchanges occur when making a donation

What are lifetime values?

Retaining customers for life is easier said than done! Marketing today is increasingly concerned with 'customer retention' (instead of just 'customer acquisition'), and customer selection (choosing and keeping only the best customers). This means keeping your best customers for life. This makes sense when you consider the value of repeat business. What do you think is the average customer lifetime value for petrol, cigarettes or office computers? How much might an average buyer buy during a lifetime? Have a guess (using today's prices).

Petrol – the average UK car driver will buy approximately £40,000 worth of petrol during 40 years of driving. Cigarettes – the average '20 a day' smoker will spend approximately £28,000 during 40 years of smoking. Office computers – the average buyer replaces/updates the system and/ or hardware every three to five years, say 10 times over 40 years which equals 10 computer systems. These are the 'lifetime values'. Profits on sales to existing customers are much higher than profits on sales to new customers (who require a lot of effort and expenditure). So lifetime customers increase sales revenues and profits. And everyone has a part to play in developing long-lasting relationships with lifetime customers.

In fact, marketing-orientated organizations do not keep marketing to themselves, ie they do not restrict marketing to the marketing department. Marketing permeates the whole organization as part of the corporate culture or corporate attitude, and as David Packard of Hewlett Packard said, 'Marketing is far too important to be left to the marketing department.' A customer focus has got to permeate every level throughout the organization. Marketing should not be an isolated department. It should integrate with all other departments, managers and staff members at every level. In reality this is a huge task. Staff need to be educated, involved, motivated and decently treated.

Happy Employees = Happy Customers and Happy Customers = Happy Shareholders. In fact, get the balance right between these three stakeholders (employees, customers and shareholders) and results will rocket! So market orientation involves everyone. But does it really happen?

Do you think that many organizations really develop a marketing orientation throughout the organization? Here is what some marketing experts think about the lack of market orientation in British companies. Professor Peter Doyle blames education, corporate cultures and the financial structures of British companies. Post Office chairman Sir Bryan

Nicholby can spot the problem just from flicking through an organization's annual report. UK market research company GALLUP have found that the lack of marketing is one of the key reasons for corporate failure.

Runaway radical retail chain proprietress Anita Roddick of the Body Shop thinks that there is a new business language that explains today's need for a fresh approach to marketing. A marketing orientation helps to develop long-term relationships with lifetime customers. Do you think many companies are truly marketing orientated?

> Happy Employees = Happy Customers and Happy Customers = Happy Shareholders.

Are markets becoming more competitive?

How's this for an aggressive competitor? *Fortune Magazine* (28 October 1996) reported that Coca-Cola's Doug Ivester urges managers to play by the rule of Ray Kroc, the founder of McDonalds (another Pepsi Co nemesis), 'What do you do when your competitor is drowning? Get a live hose and stick it in his mouth.'

Markets are becoming more competitive today than ever before. Partly because of global competition and partly because reaction times are quicker and product life cycles are shorter. No market is safe from competition.

New competitors (new entrants) emerge and establish themselves more freely as trade and technical barriers are reduced around the world. Watch how the euro (currency) increases competition as price comparisons become easier and customers gain confidence. New competitors will be pulled into new markets by customers looking for better deals. The Internet is accelerating competition as the traditional geographical boundaries disappear into the new cyber world – the new market space where competitors from anywhere in the world compete for the growing percentage of customers who buy through the Internet.

Increasing sales is a common objective among most organizations. One way of achieving this is by finding new customers who previously belonged to your competition. Similarly, somewhere out there are competitors analysing and targeting your customers as you read this page. They are, however, not always easy to see. Competition can attack an organization's sales, market share or profits directly and indirectly. A market-orientated organization continually seeks to understand (through research) customers, competitors, long-term trends and much more.

A real market-orientated organization spends time studying customers, competitors and market trends. All employees become marketing orientated. They are encouraged to develop long-lasting relationships that help to retain customers for life and to protect them from competitive temptations.

Somewhere out there, as you read this page, competitors are analysing and targeting your customers

Notes

[1]SAS Institute (1998) *Do You know Your Customer*, July (based on IT personnel in 110 blue chip companies).

[2]Flawed Web sites (1998), Port80.com (survey of 911 UK companies offering Web development).

[3]Otto, Dirk, editor *Internet World*, German edition (1998) (a survey of 50 major German companies).

[4]*The Marketing Society* (1999) 'Is British industry listening hard enough to customers?' (an electronic survey of 479 senior line marketing personnel).

[5]Ibid.

[6]Ibid.

segmentation, position and the marketing mix

- What exactly is segmentation?
- Why bother with segmentation, let's get out and sell?
- How do you segment a market?
- How do you select a target market?
- What exactly is positioning?
- How do benefits mix with positioning strategies?
- How do you develop a positioning?
- What is the marketing mix?
- What other marketing mixes exist beyond the 4Ps?
- How do you mix the mix?
- Why does the marketing mix change?

What exactly is segmentation?

A segment is a unique group of customers (or potential customers) who share some common characteristics that make them different from other groups of customers. People are different. Some segments have different needs, require different versions of the same product, pay different prices, buy in different places, can be reached by different media.

In consumer markets, customers and prospective customers can be grouped together, or 'segmented', in lots of different ways... by their age, their sex, where they live, how they live, what they earn, and so on.

In organizational markets or industrial markets, customers and prospective customers are generally segmented by the actual type of business, its size, location and even culture or how they operate. You can investigate each of these in more detail in 'How do you segment a market?' on page 26.

Customers and prospective customers can be further segmented according to whether they are heavy or light users of a particular product or service, and whether they are very loyal to a particular brand or supplier.[1]

It is worth spending time getting to know your customers. Each segment that is chosen, or targeted, needs to be treated differently in some way. Different segments often pay different prices, buy in different places, watch different media and often simply want a different product. Different segments require different solutions. Segmenting and selecting the best market segments is called target marketing. This is a vital marketing skill.

If you are going to get the best results, you must know what is happening in your marketplace. In the 1960s we had mass marketing. In the 1970s segmentation became more popular. In the 1980s target marketing became so precise that narrower, smaller segments or niche markets emerged. One-to-one marketing grew in the 1990s as technology and know-how spread, and named individuals were targeted directly through database marketing's direct mail and telesales. The marketer can now communicate with thousands, or even millions, of individually named customers. Some say that there are no more mass markets – no more masses of homogeneous customers wanting the same as everyone else.

Marketers today, can satisfy smaller and smaller segments, right down to individual requirements. In the new millennium, mass customization means that many products and services can be tailor-made in the factory to suit thousands, or even millions, of individual requirements. By the end of the 90s, Levi's, Barbie dolls, health pills and house insurance had already moved towards tailor-made mass customization.

But more than one individual is often involved in the decisions to buy, to vote or to behave in some way. For example, children influence which cereals their parents buy. The children are, in turn, influenced by their peers and 'advisers' at school and in the playground. This is where segmentation focuses on the Decision Making Unit, or DMU. Who is involved in making the final decision to buy or not to buy? The DMU is made up of starters or initiators, advisers, deciders, purchasers and end-users. DMUs are very important in organizational markets, too. For example, the marketing of a new computer system to a large industrial corporation would obviously involve several people in the final decision.[2]

So keep your eyes open and remember segmentation is a vital skill for marketers. But why is it? Why do we bother with segmentation? This question is answered on page 24.

Mass customization is here to stay

Why bother with segmentation, let's get out and sell?

Why bother segmenting markets? Think about a beautiful Rembrandt or Picasso painting for a moment. In some segments these paintings would not sell even for £50, and in the wrong age segment not even for 50p. In the right segment, a Rembrandt might fetch £50 million. Why waste your efforts on the wrong people? Why not target people who first want, and then can afford your product or service?

Segmentation and target marketing not only reduce waste, but also help to boost sales, and find the best prices. Some people are more likely to buy your product, service or idea than other people.

Time spent carefully segmenting and accurately targeting helps to find those people. Sloppy targeting, on the other hand, not only wastes resources, but it can also damage an organization's reputation. Without segmentation, the likelihood of success reduces. Careful segmentation sows the seeds of success. It is worth spending time considering who the best customers* are, what segment they are in and how to reach them.

Segmentation helps to see the target customers more effectively. If you don't know what you are aiming at how can you hit the target? Segmentation allows the marketer to break up the market, focus on the best segments and find new customers who might otherwise have been lost in a sea of faces. In a sense, segmentation forces the marketer to learn more about customers. A regular review of the market and its segments encourages the marketer to think about customers, their changing needs and circumstances. This kind of market research keeps you close to the customer, which means you are more likely to understand and satisfy the customer's needs now and in the future.

This 'closer understanding of customer needs' helps to protect an organization's existing customer base from the inevitable onslaught of competitors and their offerings. As wave after wave of competitive suppliers emerge on the global horizon, the organization that sticks closely to the customer has a better chance of keeping its customers.

Staying close to customers and responding to their changing needs helps to keep customers satisfied by identifying their needs and priorities and, subsequently, developing products and services that are required by specific customer segments. In summary, 'staying close to customers keeps customers'. Customer retention is vital, particularly as existing customers can be five times more profitable than new customers.

Identifying what each segment wants, what it can afford, whether it is loyal to a particular competitor and how it might respond to your offer is all vital information for the marketer.

Careful segmentation and accurate targeting keeps you close to the market, reduces waste, finds the best customers and helps to keep them satisfied. Segmentation can boost results, but how do you actually segment a market?

If you don't know whom you are aiming at, how can you hit the target?

---

* Best customers are those customers who really like doing business with you, who don't constantly haggle over prices, who don't just buy only when there is a special promotion, who give useful feedback, who participate in new product development – even suggest new product ideas – and who will stay loyal to you for a lifetime – if you treat them well. Not all of your customers will fit into this exclusive customer segment.

How do you segment a market?

We know that segmentation is crucial in marketing, but how do you do it? You can segment consumer markets using many different variables which include: geographic, demographic, geodemographic, psychographic and behaviour patterns.

Geographic segments mean location and this can include: streets, towns, cities, regions, countries, continents, and trading blocks like the EU and NAFTA.

Demographics, or social statistics, include: age, sex, family life cycle, and job type/socio-economic group income level.

Geodemographics mixes geographic and demographic data to create categories of house-types with locations, for example, people who live in 'detached houses in exclusive suburbs'.

Psychographics attempt to segment according to psychological profiles of people in terms of their lifestyles, attitudes and personalities, for example, 'active go-getters'.[3] And the fifth variable used when segmenting consumer markets looks at actual behaviour patterns relating to the particular product or service. Behavioural segments address behaviour patterns, which include usage (eg heavy or light users) and uses (the way a product or service is used – in other words, the benefit enjoyed). You can even segment by benefits enjoyed – different segments buy the same product for different reasons. Some people buy diet food to look good; others to live longer. Even bicycles are bought for completely different benefits (leisure and transport).[4]

Consider now industrial, organizational and business-to-business markets. These are also broken into segments. Customers' organizations are grouped by type of business, size of business, where they are located and how they operate, or their corporate culture.

Customer type categorizes the type of product or service that the customer organization produces. In the UK, industry type is defined by the SIC code (Standard Industrial Classification).

The size of the customer, in terms of sales, number of staff and usage, may determine whether it is worth targeting or not. Size of customer is also influenced by whether it is a heavy or light user of a particular product or service, and whether it is very loyal to a particular competitor. Remember that heavy users tend to be bigger customers; they also tend to attract fierce competition.

Location means physical geographic location, eg where is the factory? Location may also refer to the number and location of branches. Do local customers make better targets than distant overseas customers? Do all companies operate in global segments?

The culture, or corporate culture – this refers to the organization's values and attitudes – is it innovative or conservative? The structure – is it centralized or decentralized? Corporate culture can determine whether an organization fits into a particular segment.

Job title or job type may determine a segment. For example, an organization selling safety products would be particularly interested in targeting health and safety managers. With industrial or consumer markets, segmentation is essential, but it's not always easy. There are inevitably some complications, such as a lack of neat categories, floating targets and loyalty barriers.

Not all customers fall neatly into a single category or segment. For example, 70 per cent of buyers of the *Sun* newspaper are predominately 'C2DEs' (blue-collar workers), while 30 per cent are 'ABC1s' (white-collar workers). Despite these difficulties, it is an exercise worth regularly engaging in, as time spent segmented will be rewarded with bigger sales.

Although exhausting, time spent segmenting reaps dividends

How do you select a target market?

Once you have broken a market up into segments, the next question is: which segment is it the most attractive segment? Just like choosing a market, choosing a segment involves a lot of work. Careful analysis should reveal whether a particular segment suits the organization in terms of size, profitability, growth, competition and resources required. Let's look at each of these briefly.

- Size – this can be a delicate and difficult question. Is the segment big enough to make the effort worthwhile or profitable? Is it so big that it attracts intense competition? Is it part of a much bigger global segment?

- Profitability – can the segment be serviced within an acceptable cost level, and can it simultaneously bear a price level that generates a reasonable profit? Again, if the segment is seen to be very profitable, it will attract a lot of competition.

- Growth – is the segment in the decline or growth phase of its product life cycle?

- Competition – direct and indirect, local and international, now and in the future? Can the organization compete?

- The resources required – this means whether the organization is capable of creating, communicating and delivering a specific type or range of products, or services, at a particular price to a particular segment. Ideally, the organization should have a distinctive sustainable competence (compared to the competition) in at least one of these areas.

The next question is: what broad strategy should be used? Three common strategies are:

- Undifferentiated marketing – the mass marketing approach that ignores differences among segments.

- Differentiated – this is where an organization operates in two or more segments by offering different marketing mixes for each segment.

- Concentrated marketing – this focuses one marketing mix in just one segment.

Breaking markets into relevant segments and selecting the best targets depend on what you believe makes a segment worth targeting. Ideally the segment's purchasing criteria should match the organization's offering (marketing mix). On the other hand, when selecting a segment, different organizations have different criteria, but size, profitability, growth, competition and resources required are commonly used as segment selection criteria.

The Eskimo Story
Two Eskimos broke a hole in the ice and dropped a fishing line down. After an hour or so, a voice boomed out from up high 'There ain't no fish down there!' So they pulled up the line and marched across the ice for another 50 metres, broke a hole and dropped a line. After another hour, the same voice rang out 'There ain't no fish down there!' The younger one, although brave, nervously shouted upwards 'Oh, who is it that speaks to us from on high?' After a pause the voice boomed 'The ice rink manager!'

Moral: If there ain't no fish in the pond, don't fish there... wrong targets are a waste of time.

What exactly is positioning?

Positioning is all about how a brand or company is positioned or perceived in the minds of a target group of customers. Perceptual maps help us to plan positionings and repositionings.

A perceptual map is a diagram that plots different positionings and repositionings. For example, Guinness was positioned as an 'old un-fashionable mature drinker's drink' in the 1970s. Demographic shifts resulting from the 60s baby boom meant that in the early 80s Guinness was wrongly positioned for the booming younger beer market. With the help of a new advertising campaign, it repositioned itself from old and unfashionable to young and fashionable. Sales grew immediately. As the market leaves the 90s and moves into the second millennium, watch how Guinness repositions itself in tune with market changes.

Lucozade was repositioned from a sick child's drink to a healthy adult's drink in the faster growing healthy adults' soft-drink sector. The company saw a bigger target market in the faster growing healthy adults' soft-drink market and it repositioned the brand accordingly. Could you plot the old positioning?

It changed the advertising, the packaging and expanded the distribution channels beyond chemist shops. In short, it changed the marketing mix and targeted a new sector – the soft-drinks' market. This radical reposi-tioning helped sales to grow.

So brands can be repositioned if accompanied by changes in target markets, which usually means changing the marketing mix in some way. The marketing mix is dealt with in more detail separately in this book. For now, it is worth remembering that everything a company does can affect the positioning of its products in the minds of its customers.

The product, or service itself, the way it is presented and promoted, delivered and even the prices that are charged – these are all part of the marketing mix – which, in turn, affects the way a product or service is perceived or positioned in the minds of people. Today, the company behind the brand also affects the brand's positioning (as the image of the holding companies, eg Shell or Nestlé, can influence how their individual brands are perceived or positioned).

The selection of target markets also affects the positioning. For instance, a soft drink targeted at teenagers and a soft drink targeted at senior citizens would by association with its users generate very different positionings.

Effective positioning, therefore, requires an in-depth understanding of the market, its needs, its segments and the target markets selected.

When developing a positioning strategy consider whether the organization can provide something that is: first, required by the market; second, distinctive; and finally, sustainable? Can the organization provide the resources to support and sustain the desired positioning? How to develop a positioning is a different question and is duly addressed on page 34.

Lucozade was positioned as a sick child's drink

Lucozade is now repositioned as a healthy adult's drink

How do benefits mix with positioning strategies?

Positioning is central to marketing strategy. Positioning means how a product or service is positioned or perceived in the minds of customers within the target market. Marketers try to establish a particular desired positioning for their product or service.

For example, some brands of holidays are specifically positioned as 'young and exciting', while others are positioned as 'mature and conservative'.

Some brands change their positioning as they move into different markets. As mentioned on page 30, Lucozade was once positioned as a sick child's drink. After many years it was repositioned as a healthy adult's drink suitable for the growing healthy adults' market.

Before developing a clear positioning, you need to consider some fundamental questions. What is the market? What does it want? What benefits are bought?

Black and Decker drills are in the drill market. Or are they? Do people buy drills because they want a drill? No. They buy drills because they want holes. So they are buying hole-makers. People want reliable, easy hole-makers – drills that make hole-making ever so easy.

Further research into the male segment exploring what men want when they buy a drill may reveal that some men want to be the complete man – complete with full armoury of DIY equipment, and Black and Decker can deliver this emotional satisfaction. Another segment, female drill buyers, on the other hand, may want drills for immediate results. Purely functional.

Examining the market, the benefits sought and the benefits that can be provided give some useful clues as to how the product might be positioned in the first place. For example, should the Black and Decker be positioned as a highly functional tool or as part of the complete man's kit? And what about the female buyer? Should it be positioned differently for different segments? Or would this cost too much money? Would it dilute the message and cause confusion? This is an important strategic decision that needs careful attention. Perceptual maps help to plan positioning strategies. Perceptual maps, positioning and repositioning and differential advantage are considered in 'What exactly is positioning?' on page 30.

Do customers buy drills, hole-makers, macho makers or secure jobs?

How do you develop a positioning?

Positioning is a very important aspect of marketing. There are many different variables that can be used to position a new brand, or reposition an old brand. Some positioning variables are more appropriate than others. Some variables are more attractive to the target market than others.

The first question is – what does the market want? Then, what do target customers want? What is their ideal brand? These questions provide answers that help to identify the ideal positioning? But can the organization fulfil the ideal positioning? Has it got the resources? Is it capable of continually delivering a suitable marketing mix? For example, can we deliver an upmarket product? Can we manufacture high-quality products in the first place?

Then ask, is a particular positioning very cluttered with competition or should we look for an unoccupied position which is both attractive to the customer and sustainable in the future? What are the variables that create positionings?

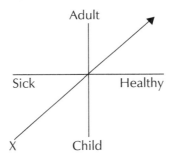

Page 30 showed how Lucozade used age (young and old) and health/ lifestyle (as well as sick and healthy) as the relevant positioning variables. Guinness used age and fashion. There are many other variables that create perceptions or positionings.

American academics Aaker and Shansby[5] categorized all the variables into six groups as follows:

■ Attribute, eg gentleness, ruggedness, tasteful.

- Price and quality, eg premium-quality image or value-based.
- Use or application, eg associations with a particular situation or occasion for use.
- User, eg linking the product or service to types of users, lifestyles, profiles.
- Product class, eg positioning in diet foods or in normal foods.
- Competitor, eg positioning against a competitor – Avis, 'we try harder' – and competitive advertising.

Positioning is a key part of marketing. It requires an in-depth understanding of markets, segments, targets, competition and the organization's resources. Positioning is inextricably linked to target markets and segmentation. Successful positioning, or repositioning as in the case of Guinness and Lucozade, can really help to boost sales, market share and overall results.

"Positioning is key to marketing strategy."

Professor Peter Doyle Marketing CD ROM Title 2,
Segmentation, Positioning and the Marketing Mix,
The Multimedia Marketing Consortium 1996.

What is the marketing mix?

What exactly is the marketing mix? It is a framework that helps to structure the approach to each market. The mix is a bundle of controllable variables that are offered to (and influence) the customer. These variables include: the product or service itself – its advantages; its availability – the place where and when it is available, delivered or distributed; its image – the way it is promoted; and, of course, the price that should be charged.

These are some of the ingredients (the 4Ps) that a marketing manager must mix together when optimizing a limited amount of resources. In 1960, Jerome McCarthy presented the 4Ps to the world. Since then marketing managers around the world have become familiar with them. Product, Price, Place, and Promotion. In addition to the 4Ps, there are other approaches to the mix (particularly the service mix/7Ps) and these are explored under the heading 'What other marketing mixes exist beyond the 4Ps' on page 38. For now, consider each of the 4Ps briefly.

Product – this means the product's (or service's) quality, the functions, the features and benefits of its design plus packaging, guarantees and level of after-sales service. Choices can be made about any of these aspects.

Price – includes recommended prices to end-user customers, distributors' trade prices, cash discounts, bulk discounts and terms of credit.

Place – where and when the customer buys and consumes the product or service. Place is sometimes referred to as the marketing channels, physical distribution, logistics or location.

Promotion – the promotions mix or the communications mix. This mix includes advertising, sales promotions, publicity, direct mail, exhibitions, display, packaging, selling and even word-of-mouth.

What is the best mix? A marketing manager has to juggle resources and decide on the best marketing mix. Should money be spent or forfeited on: reduced prices; improved products; new delivery trucks? Or maybe invest all your money in a high-risk TV-advertising campaign? In addition, the choice of target market affects the mix. Professor Philip Kotler wrote:

'For example, in India, you sell one cigarette at a time, not a package so there is a lot of localization. The biggest mistake companies make often is to assume that how they sell a product in their own country is the way to put it into another.'

So the mix must adapt itself to the needs of the market. The 4Ps, however, is just one approach to the marketing mix. You can now explore some other approaches on the next page.

Each element of the marketing mix must support the overall positioning. Here the high price tag does not match the low quality, therefore disaster

What other marketing mixes exist beyond the 4Ps?

The 4Ps is just one approach to the marketing mix. There are many other approaches.

Philip Kotler, an american author, prefers the 4Cs. He suggests that the 4Ps are a seller's mix or sales-orientated approach and it therefore should be replaced by the 4Cs which are more customer-orientated, or marketing-orientated.

- Product = Customer benefits
- Price = Cost to customer
- Place = Convenience
- Promotion = Communications

Going back to the 4Ps, some feel this approach to the marketing mix misses the most important part of marketing – the centre of the marketing universe is omitted. What is the centre of the marketing universe? The 5th P is 'People' – customers and employees. Customers are at the centre of the marketing universe. However, 'people' in the context of the marketing mix generally mean employees.

Now lets move on to the 7Ps. Although the 4Ps can be used for both products and services, some feel that the 4Ps works better for products than it does for services.

American academics Booms and Bitner[6] felt that the 7Ps are more appropriate for the service sector such as hotels or transport companies. Four of the 7Ps are the same. Product, Price, Place and Promotion. Can you guess what the others might be?

People, Process and Physical evidence. Each of these Ps affects what the customer is offered.

- People are employees.
- Process means the production and delivery of the service.
- Physical evidence means the interior and exterior of the buildings (signage, livery, staff uniforms, etc).

In 1961, Albert Frey[7] suggested that all the marketing mix variables could be categorized into just two groups:

- The offering
- The methods and tools

The offering consisted of product, packaging, service, brand and price, while the methods and tools included distribution channels, personal selling, advertising and sales promotion.

So there are several different ways of categorizing the mix. There are also several different ways of mixing the mix. Should advertising be increased, prices slashed, deliveries reduced and products upgraded? Or the other way around? You can explore this in the next section called 'How do you mix the mix?'

The marketing mix has definitely not got anything to do with an over zealous bunch of marketing professionals based in Ireland.

How do you mix the mix?

There is no one single perfect marketing mix. Some mixes are, however, better than others. The marketing mix has an infinite amount of combinations or mixes. The same product can have extremely different mixes for different market segments around the world.

Ranges of prices, distribution options, product modifications and pro-motional strategies can all be mixed in different ways. They should, however, fit together to consolidate a single desired positioning in a particular market segment.

The mix should not pull in different directions, for example, a high price for low-quality goods does not make sense in the long-term repeat-business world of relationship marketing. Equally – low-quality, discount-priced products will find distribution in a luxury upmarket store difficult to achieve.

Here is a new product. Market it. Mix the mix.

A friend's mother has developed a watch which has a videophone and magnifying glass for viewing. A combination of miniaturization and micro chips means the video watch can be produced for as little as £2.00 per unit. She has asked you to help her to draw up an outline marketing mix. Consider two different mixes. What would you do? The first question to ask is, what is the market? Then, what benefits does this product deliver? Who might enjoy these benefits. Next, consider various segments and possible target markets that would also help. A clear view on the positioning also helps. An understanding of what resources the company has would be vital.

One option would be to recommend a retail price for the video phone watch of £1,000, distribute it through luxury stores like Harrods and Neiman and Marcus and promote it with elaborate in-store displays (merchandising) supported with a limited mail shot and PR campaign. Now consider another option. This time change the marketing mix radically. Reduce the price and sell it in packs of two through a discount warehouse supported by a national TV-advertising campaign.

Each ingredient in the mix can vary enormously, eg the watch can be made out of plastic or platinum. It can have a lifetime guarantee or become a disposable product. It can have lots of extras, such as diamond studded leather straps, silk wrapping, guarantees, etc. On the other hand, it can have no added costs and no added extras – just the basic video watch.

These are decisions which the marketing manager has to make after careful analysis of the situation, the markets, its needs, its sectors, the ideal positioning, the resources within the company. So is there a single perfect marketing mix? No, although, some mixes are obviously better than others.

Finally, some countries require different mixes. Some segments require different mixes within the same country. The mix can change according to market requirements, which in themselves change over time. The ever-changing mix is discussed on page 42.

There is more than one way to market a product

Why does the marketing mix change?

An excellent marketing mix in one period may not be as effective in another period. The marketing mix changes over time. Partly because markets change, new sectors evolve, trends develop, attitudes change, different ideal positionings emerge, technology moves on, new products arrive, different distribution channels appear.

Just look at the personal computer, or PC, market. Today's PCs are better products, have much lower prices and different methods of distribution compared with 10 years ago. Today, thousands of people buy PCs through mail order. Ten years ago this would never have been the case.

The marketing mix has to change to meet new market conditions. Here is an example of how different elements of the marketing mix dominated the retail petrol market in the UK over a period of time. In the early 1960s, product performance – miles per gallon and reliability were very important. Then the marketing emphasis switched to promotions with the Green Shield Stamps war in the late 1960s. Physical distribution and sourcing of supplies became vital during the first oil crisis in 1973. This was followed by a price war in 1974 that was in turn followed by supply and distribution during the second oil crisis in 1979. The early 80s saw location and design of new retail sites as the key to competitive advantage. This was followed by the mid-80s sales promotions war as petrol retailers competed to give away instant gifts, tokens, scratch cards. These sales promotions were supported by large advertising budgets. So now the advertising promoted the sales promotions rather than the product itself. Some advertising campaigns even advertised the fact that their competitors had inferior sales promotions. In the second millennium more partnership and alliances will emerge in forecourts and supermarkets. The marketing mix can change over time. It can also change over distance.

This is particularly true in international markets, where certain approaches to advertising and promotions are acceptable in some countries but not in others, or where the distribution network is restricted or where the price structure is totally different. The optimum mix is influenced by the company's long-term policy on repeat sales, its positioning strategy, the target market selection, the firm's resources, levels of competition and the ability or willingness to change the mix according to a particular market's requirements.

Finally, the ideal mix should support the ideal positioning in the most attractive target markets.

Constant change:

"You cannot step twice into the same river for fresh waters are ever flowing in upon you."

Heraclitus, the Greek philosopher, AD *500*

Notes

[1]You can use the video browser in Marketing CD ROM Title 2: Segmentation, Positioning and the Marketing Mix (Multimedia Marketing Consortium, London) later to find out what Harvard's Professor Rosabeth Moss Kanter thinks about loyalty segments.

[2]Marketing managers talk about DMUs in the video browser in Marketing CD ROM Title 2: Segmentation, Positioning and the Marketing Mix, Multimedia Marketing Consortium, London.

[3]You can use the video browser in Marketing CD ROM Title 2: Segmentation, Positioning and the Marketing Mix (Multimedia Marketing Consortium, London) later to find out what Professor Peter Doyle thinks about lifestyle segments.

[4]The video browser in Marketing CD ROM Title 2: Segmentation, Positioning and the Marketing Mix (Multimedia Marketing Consortium, London) reveals Professor Philip Kotler talking about different bicycle benefits around the world.

[5]Aaker, D and Shansby, J G (1982) Position your product, *Business Horizons*, May–June, pp 56–62.

[6]Booms, B H and Bitner, M J (1981) Marketing strategies and organizational structures for service firms, in *Marketing of Services*, ed J Donnelly and W George, pp 47–51, American Marketing Association, Chicago.

[7]Frey, A (1961) *Advertising*, 3rd edn, Ronald Press, New York.

three

marketing
planning

- Why bother planning?
- How do marketing plans and corporate plans fit together?
- What are the three key resources?
- What should be in the perfect marketing plan?
- What needs to be analysed?
- What are good marketing objectives?
- What exactly is strategy?
- What is the difference between strategy and tactics?
- How do you implement tactical decisions?
- Do we really need a review?
- Does SOSTAC work?

Why bother planning?

Planning. It's a pain in the neck! It takes too much time. And time is what I don't have. I need to be out there with my customers. Or so some managers say. Good marketers stick close to their customers – they don't hide behind desks in ivory towered offices... planning! But wait a minute, how much money is needed for advertising and promotions? How much stock is required? Is there money available for a new brochure? Will it be ready for the exhibition? Without a plan there is no control, just different people pushing in different directions. Without a plan, you lose control, and in some cases, you lose your business. For example, some organizations have big increases in sales and profits, but still go out of business. Why? Because of the cash flow problems caused by unplanned growth or 'overtrading'. Sales and marketing must integrate with other functions such as finance.

Excellent marketing managers always write carefully researched marketing plans. But this does take time. However, planning also saves the time that would be wasted by the confusion and chaos generated when there is no planned approach. Decisions made under chaotic conditions are rarely clearly thought out and are therefore more prone to error. Foreword planning reduces the stress and panic that thrive when rushed decisions have to be made without reference to any overall plan. By thinking ahead and planning ahead many problems are solved long before they ever occur. Planning reduces mistakes that inevitably cost time and money. Planning stops the fire fighting and spots what starts the fire before it ignites. Looking into the future can help managers to recognize the hidden opportunities and threats that lie on the horizon. The planning process also identifies the winning strengths, which can be built upon, and weaknesses, which need to be minimized.

Planning forces the manager to consider the future... even create the future! This is vital. Managers need to move away occasionally from the day-to-day operations and reflect on the bigger picture – how it all fits together. This, in turn, helps to improve communications and share responsibilities as it identifies who needs to do what and when.

Plans offer a mechanism for integrating activities at different levels. For example, plans help to ensure that marketing integrates with business functions such as production and finance. Planning also helps the marketing mix to integrate and work together instead of pulling in different directions; for example, each element of the mix should reinforce the planned 'positioning'. Forward planning encourages integrated communications.

This further strengthens the image and simultaneously saves money on communications tools such as advertising, direct mail and promotions, and can, if carefully planned, convey a consistent message by using some common images across advertising, direct mail, promotions, packaging, point-of-sale, exhibitions and sales conferences. Costs are cut as some creative work on photographs and illustrations can be reduced. The savings are even greater for pan-European and for global marketers.

Planning saves money and a planned approach avoids paying 'rush rates', higher prices to photographers, designers, printers, the media and so on. The more notice or time they are given, the less money they charge. Some printers, for example, give extra discounts on jobs that are booked months in advance. It's the same with anything. If you are desperate and a job is urgent, you will pay more money. Think of your own local plumber – emergencies cost more than a scheduled or planned service. Time is money – the shorter it is, the more you pay.

Planning – along with leading, organizing and controlling – is one of the key skills that a manager must have. In fact, they are linked: unless you have a plan it is difficult to lead, to organize or to control.

To summarize, planning saves time and money, reduces stress, panic and heart attacks, paints a bigger picture, looks to the future, stops constant fire fighting, integrates activities, helps a manager to lead, organize and control effectively.

Planning stops heart attacks, saves money and paints a bigger picture

How do marketing plans and corporate plans fit together?

The corporate plan is the big plan that directs all the organization's functions, resources and activities. Marketing plans, along with production plans or operation plans, human resource plans and financial plans, should integrate with each other and fit with the overall direction of the corporate plan. One area where corporate plans and marketing plans overlap is the mission statement. This is a concisely written statement that defines which business the organization is in, in terms of customer needs, and what are the organization's goals and values. Great management thinkers like Levitt and Drucker cite inadequate missions as a key reason for failure.

Corporate plans tend to concern longer term, bigger issues. This includes major investments and major divestments – which markets, products and technologies to invest in? And which to get out of? Corporate plans help to decide whether growth can be achieved organically from within the organization, through sales of existing products, the launching of new products or finding new markets? Or can growth be achieved externally through acquisitions, mergers and strategic alliances with other organizations?

At each level in an organization, managers make plans. There is a hierarchy of plans. At the top level, the board of directors agree the overall corporate strategy or corporate plan. Below the board, marketing directors and managers make their own detailed plans covering their specific products and markets.

In larger organizations, the marketing director may have group product managers who are responsible for several different products, brands or markets. Each of these group product managers may have, in turn, several different brand managers reporting to him or her.

Should planning be top down or bottom up? Should top management create plans without input from the managers below? Or should plans be written by lower level managers, added together and delivered as the corporate plan? In reality it is a bit of both – all levels have to be involved. The corporate plan may have a longer time horizon than the marketing plan. But even marketing plans have different time horizons. Long term, in European and US businesses, generally means anywhere from 5 years onwards. Medium term means 2–4 years and short term generally means one year. The short-term orientation of these Western businesses creates a serious disadvantage when competing against the long-term orientation of the Pacific Rim businesses. Short termism forces a business into short-term relations with customers. This breeds 'transactional marketing' or a single short-term sale rather than developing longer-term 'relationship marketing'. This strategy of relationship marketing builds repeat business over many years.

And one man's strategy is another man's objective. Remember the hierarchy of planning? There is also a hierarchy of objectives. A higher level strategy becomes a lower level objective. For example, the corporate objective might be to increase return on investment by strategically becoming the cost leader with mass-volume, low-cost products. This affects many functional managers such as production and marketing. Take marketing, this mass-volume, low-cost strategy now becomes the marketing manager's objective. This might be achieved by a major sales drive to expand the number of distributors. This marketing strategy now becomes the sales manager's objective, which might be achieved with a sales strategy that recruits and trains a bigger and better sales force.

If the plan is not delivering the required results – it needs to be changed. Plans should be flexible. Annual plans are typically reviewed each quarter, while medium to long-term plans are reviewed each year.

Contingency plans need to be prepared in case things go wrong. So all plans are but snapshots in time. Unless they are flexible and revised regularly, they will probably fail. As the Scottish poet Robert Burns said, 'The best laid plans of mice and men gang aft aglay.' The trick of planning is to keep it current and revised as conditions change. Then it cannot go astray and will not 'gang aft aglay'.

The marketing plan must integrate and fit with the overall direction of the bigger corporate plan

What are the three key resources?

A marketing plan must specify the resources required to do the job. Here is a simple aide-mémoire that you can use as a checklist when writing or reviewing marketing plans – the 3Ms. Every plan must have the 3Ms. If a plan has not got the 3Ms, then it is unprofessional and incomplete as these are three vital resources that all good plans use throughout.

- Men mean men and women – the human resource.
- Money means budgets – how much will it all cost?
- Minutes mean time – the most limited resource.

Men means men and women. Will an in-house team do it or will an outside agency handle it? Do you need a telesales team? Are there enough delivery drivers? Who can handle the running of an exhibition, a sales conference or a product launch? Who will do the marketing research? Do you need to recruit some graduates as marketing assistants? Who will do what? Has the marketing team got enough skills? Some feel that an organization's greatest assets walk out the door each night – the staff. Are they happy? Will they come back tomorrow, next month, next year, next project?

Money – marketing costs money. How much should you spend? Is it money well spent? Can you measure the effectiveness or productivity of various marketing activities? Can you measure the return or profit generated by marketing activities? What will be the effect on the cash flow of the business? Is cash available? Will the board approve the budget request? There are many ways of building a marketing budget. With experience, budgeting gets easier. But always remember to put some money into a contingency budget for the unexpected. Marketing plans must include money. Financial figures include expenditures as well as sales, costs, contribution and net profits. Return on investment can be calculated on certain marketing activities such as direct mail or exhibitions. Numbers cannot be avoided in a marketing plan. Forecast sales are usually a core part of the marketing plan. Sales forecasts provide crucial information for cash flow planning, production planning and, of course, marketing planning. There are many forecasting techniques, some more sophisticated than others. A simple bottom-up approach to sales forecasting is often used in conjunction with more sophisticated top-down computer-based forecasting models. Bottom up, in this case, means that each sales representative calculates what they think they can sell. The sales manager then adds them all together to get one approach to sales forecasting. The plan must have figures which are translated into finances or money.

Finally, the third M, minutes. Minutes mean time. Time is often the most limited of all the resources. Sometimes there are just not enough hours in the day, or days in the week! It's not surprising that time management courses are so popular today. Time is a scarce resource. You need at least three months to prepare a new TV-advertising campaign, or to develop a new mail shot; it might take 12 months to create a new pack, while a new product takes a lot longer. The clothes you wear are made from fabrics designed at least three years ago. If you want to launch a new toy for Christmas, you have to exhibit it 10 months prior at the February toy fairs. A Christmas launch needs to be planned maybe three years earlier. Or have you already run out of time? Time is a limited resource that is used in different ways.[1]

So marketing plans must have timescales, deadlines and schedules. They also have to have budgets and talk in numbers. And of course, the plan should specify who does what, when. Men, money and minutes. Every plan must have them. Some say that there are other Ms such as materials and machinery. But other organizations and every marketing plan must at least include the 3Ms – men, money and minutes.

3Ms: men (and women), money (budgets) and minutes (time)
– three key resources

What should be in the perfect marketing plan?

There are many different approaches to building a marketing plan. There is no single common approach. But there are essential elements that every marketing plan must have. The SOSTAC planning system covers them all. It took me five years to devise SOSTAC, but you can learn it in five minutes. Use it and you are well on your way to building a well-structured and comprehensive plan. You can also use this approach to check other plans to see if they are comprehensive and cover the key items that every plan needs.

S   stands for Situation analysis, which means where are we now?
O   stands for Objectives, which means where do we want to go?
S   stands for Strategy, which summarizes how we are going to get there.
T   s tands for Tactics, which are the details of strategy.
A   is for Action or implementation – putting the plan to work.
C   is for Control, which means measurement, monitoring, reviewing, updating and modifying.

Add in the 3Ms – the three key resources, men, money and minutes. Men meaning men and women, expertise and abilities to do different jobs. Money means budgets – have we the money? Minutes mean time – what are the timescales, schedules or deadlines? Is there enough time? Each of the six elements of SOSTAC are considered in much greater detail elsewhere in this book.

If you can remember SOSTAC + 3Ms and build them into your marketing plan, you have the platform for writing a good marketing plan. In fact, you have an outline marketing plan. Here is what some experts feel about SOSTAC. Professor Philip Kotler, 'SOSTAC is a system for going through the steps and building a marketing plan.' Sam Howe, Director of CATV Marketing SouthWestern Bell, 'SOSTAC is a great approach for anyone going ahead and building a marketing plan.' David Solomon, Marketing Director, TVX, 'It appears that we are following the principles of SOSTAC.' John Leftwick, Marketing Director, Microsoft UK, 'We use SOSTAC within our own marketing planning.' Peter Liney, Concorde Marketing Manager, 'I think SOSTAC is very good in terms of identifying, if you like, major component parts of what you're doing in marketing.'

One question – where would you put target markets, marketing mix and positioning in SOSTAC? Target markets pop up almost everywhere! Target markets are so important that once you have identified them in the objectives, they pop up all over a marketing plan – in the situation analysis, objectives, strategy, tactics, and so on. A summary of the current marketing mix and positioning will appear in the situation analysis under a 'review' section. The future mix and positioning and target markets are often summarized under strategy and explained in detail under tactics.

SOSTAC + 3Ms = The perfect plan.

What needs to be analysed?

An analysis of the current situation is a fundamental part of the planning process. It tells you 'where you are now'. You can then decide 'where you want to go'. Deciding how you get there is another thing altogether – that's down to strategy.

First, the situation needs to be analysed both internally and externally. The internal analysis includes the organization and its performance. The external analysis looks outside the organization – at the variables beyond the organization's direct control. The internal analysis looks at key performance indicators, like sales market share, profitability, customer loyalty scores, number of new products, and so on. The performance should be measured over time, ie over a period of years. This allows the organization to see the trend – whether things are improving or declining. Numbers on their own are useless. We need to know what they mean. So try this....

Sales of £1 million. Is this good or bad news? Do we all celebrate or wait for redundancy? It depends on, firstly, the trend and, secondly, on whether the original objective was met. Thirdly, how does the performance compare to that of the competition? Even if the £1 million sales represented a fall in sales this might still be a relatively good performance if the total market shrank and several competitors went into liquidation. So we need comparative figures. Absolute and relative performance may paint different pictures. The analysis should be thorough – we also need to know why. Why are we succeeding or why are we failing? Then we can maximize success and minimize failure?

We also need to look at strengths and weaknesses compared to the competition. Is our location more convenient? Our service friendlier? Our delivery faster? Our product better or cheaper? What about 'positioning' – is the organization, or brand, perceived well? Is its reputation a strength or a weakness? Is it an asset or a liability? What is our competitive advantage? Can we keep it up? Is it sustainable? This is a vital question: what is our sustainable competitive advantage? Can the competition copy us? What is the long-term difference between winners and losers in our market? What are the key success factors? Do we have them? Can we protect them? These strengths and weaknesses are controllable variables because management can generally change them if, firstly, it decides to do so, and, secondly, it has access to the necessary resources... the 3Ms – men, money and minutes (see page 50).

The identification of the internal strengths and weaknesses is part of a SWOT analysis... strengths, weaknesses, opportunities and threats. The 'OT' looks out at the variables in the external environment that can affect a business. These are generally beyond its direct control. The external environment can be categorized in different ways. The far environment includes the STEP 1 variables: social, technical, economic and political (these are also called PEST factors). The near environment is closer to the organization and includes STEP 2 variables: structure of the industry, trends in the market, microeconomics and power forces shaping the industry. Some managers include competitor analysis and customer analysis in STEP 2, others analyse them separately. The analysis has to be carried out regularly because everything changes. Customers grow old and die. Market structures change. Another question which some smart organizations include in their reviews is 'learnings' – what are the five most important facts, trends or changes that have been learnt during the previous planning period? Excellent marketers constantly seek to learn from their experiences and to improve on their performances. The Japanese refer to continuous year-to-year improvement as 'kaizen'.

Internal analysis, external analysis, far and near environments, STEP, SWOT, the competition, customers, key performance indicators and learnings provide a good structure for a situation analysis. Now that you know 'where you are', you can decide 'where you want to go'. The next section on 'objectives' considers this in more detail.

An analysis of the current situation tells you 'where you are now'

What are good marketing objectives?

The situation analysis basically asks 'Where are we now?', the objectives ask 'Where do we want to go?', and the strategy summarizes 'How we are going to get there'. Let's look at where we want to go – the objectives. Many different kinds of objectives appear in marketing plans. It depends on the organization, its size and structure. There are two types of objectives that commonly appear and these are marketing objectives and communication objectives.

Typically, marketing objectives refer to sales, market share, customer satisfaction, customer retention, distribution penetration, number of new products launched, profitability, and so on. An Ansoff matrix can help to categorize types of marketing objectives such as increasing sales in an existing market, expanding into a new market, developing a new product or diversifying altogether. But are these objectives? What's missing? Numbers. Ideally, objectives should have numbers. They should be quantified so that they can be compared to actual results later in the year. For example, 'increasing sales' is too vague. By how much and when? Objectives should also have a deadline.[2] Here are some simple examples. To increase sales of the *Daily Planet* by 10 per cent within 6 months, or to increase distribution penetration of the *Daily Planet* from 25 per cent to 35 per cent of all independently owned newsagents within 12 months. But even for Superman, are these objectives realistic? Are the 3M resources available – men, money and minutes? The Resources section in this book goes into this in more detail.

The marketing objectives may also be underpinned by financial objectives relating to levels of profit, margins, contribution, break-even and, very often, cash flow. The second kind of objective found in marketing plans are communications objectives. These generally refer to the state of mind of the target market. For example, to reposition Lucozade from a sick child's drink to a healthy adult's drink over an 18-month period. AIDA is one of many communications models which are sometimes used to help to write meaningful communications objectives. AIDA stands for attention, interest, desire and action. This suggests that customers have to move through a series of mental states before they buy. Objectives can be built around these. Awareness is commonly used, but 'to increase awareness' is not an adequate objective.

Why? Numbers: it must be quantifiable to be measurable. Can you think of some real communications objectives?

Here are some professional communications objectives:

- To increase awareness of Shiny Shampoo among Swedish teenage girls from 48 per cent to 60 per cent by the end of the 12-week advertising campaign.
- Or to make Gold Blend Butter to be considered as the preferred brand among 60 per cent of 18–35-year-old housewives living in Sydney within 12 months.
- Or to ensure that 50 per cent of buyers of airport de-icing chemicals include ABC brand in their tender list.

Whether marketing or communications objectives, here is a tip for writing good ones. Objectives should be SMART... that is specific, measurable, achievable, realistic and time related. So after objectives comes the most interesting bit – the strategy, ' how do we get there?' The strategy section looks at this in more detail. For now, just remember that objectives should be SMART.

Finally, there are other objectives such as 'survival' or 'to create lifetime employment' and 'to improve community involvement'. These tend to be outside of the marketing plan and may be part of the overall corporate mission.

> If you don't know where you're going (no objectives), you'll never get there.

What exactly is strategy?

Strategy summarizes how objectives will be achieved. Remember SOSTAC? SOS stands for situation analysis, objectives, strategy. The situation analysis basically asks 'Where are we now?', the objectives ask 'Where do we want to go?', and the strategy summarizes 'How we are going to get there.' Strategy is a word that generates much confusion because different people use it in different ways. And of course, there are different levels of strategy. For example, corporate strategy, marketing strategy, advertising strategy, creative strategy and media strategy. Regardless of level, strategy can be defined as the overall direction which summarizes how all the detailed tactics achieve a specific objective.

Strategies are chosen from a range of carefully considered strategic options. American author Michael Porter identified some core generic business strategic options: cost, differentiation and focus. This means you can choose whether to compete on price, or differences in the features and benefits of your product, or you can compete by focusing on specific target markets and serving them better than anyone else. Here is an example of three competitors with three different strategies in the tyre market. Goodyear chose a strategy of mass-volume, low-cost market leadership. Michelin chose a product development strategy and invested in new technology (research and development) to develop the radial tyre – this eventually redefined customer needs and made the cross-ply tyre obsolete. Armstrong Rubber adopted a third strategy – exploiting specialist application by focusing on special tyres for agricultural, aviation and civil engineering market segments.

Marketing strategy is all about segmentation and positioning, and picking the right marketing mix.

You can, of course, have more than one strategy. Here's Microsoft Marketing Director, John Leftwich, 'If our goal is to achieve a certain level of market share within a product category we could decide that, let's say we needed to achieve 50 per cent market share. We could determine that our strategy would be to get 25 per cent of that market share by encouraging new people to buy spread sheets. So we would grow the overall market and consequently achieve 25 per cent of market share. To secure the other 25 per cent of the market share our strategy could be to progressively attack one of our competitors' customer bases and encourage them to move from their product to our own. So, you can build up therefore two different strategies. One of market expansion and creation of demand and the other of a competitive stand point encouraging brands which are within a competitors' base.'

There is one important question that influences the choice of strategies, 'Does it develop and exploit our sustainable competitive advantage?' Which strategy exploits our competitive strengths, or our competitive advantage? Is this advantage sustainable in the future or will competition eat away at this temporary advantage. The key term here is sustainable competitive advantage. Do we know what it is and do the strategies exploit it? A typical competitive advantage might be better designed products, or perhaps more cost-efficient production, or better customer service, or brand imagery.

Perhaps the easiest way of understanding strategy is to say it's a summary of how you are going to achieve the objectives – it drives and summarizes the tactics. It's the big picture. It often pans over a longer period of time than shorter-term tactical activities. The choice of strategy is influenced firstly, by objectives, and secondly, by the resources available. For example, developing superior products depends on having excellent research and development facilities and people, or at least it depends on having the money to buy the facilitates and also the time to recruit and build a R&D team.

So the dimensions of marketing strategy can include objectives and resources, the scale of operation, a summary of marketing mixes, positioning, target markets and timing – do we want to be 'first to market' or come in later with a 'me too' product? Finally, strategy and tactics have military meanings. It's no coincidence that there are several books written on marketing warfare.

> **"**Therefore those who are not entirely aware of strategies that are disadvantageous, cannot be fully aware of strategies that are advantageous.**"**
>
> *Sun Tzu, c 300 BC*

What is the difference between strategy and tactics?

The SOS in SOSTAC stands for situation analysis, objectives and strategy. The TAC in SOSTAC stands for tactics, action and control. Let's look at tactics – the details of strategy. Strategy summarizes how to achieve objectives in general terms – the big picture. Tactics, on the other hand, address all the smaller detailed decisions regarding the marketing mix and target markets.

Here's Professor Peter Doyle, 'finally come the tactics which really is about the marketing mix. What pricing policy should you follow, what product range you're going to need, how should you advertise and promote the product, what distribution channels shall you need'.

Tactics tend to be short term and more flexible, while strategy is longer term and more enduring. Tactics should only really emerge after the strategy has been agreed. Ideally, tactics are developed towards the end of the marketing planning process, that is, after rather than before strategy has been agreed. Unfortunately, this is not always the case. Sometimes, bright tactical ideas drive some organizations from situation to situation without first considering the bigger picture, the overall strategic direction.

Bright ideas are fine as long as they fit into and contribute towards a sensible longer-term strategy. Tactics should not drive strategy since tactics have a shorter-term vision than strategy. An organization should not rely on short-term tactics to solve long-term problems. Most customers offer long-term opportunities of repeat business. Short-term tactics will not build long-term relationships and will not achieve relationship marketing.

Understand the difference between short- and long-term time horizons and you get a lot closer to understanding the difference between strategy and tactics. Short-term transactions do not provide long-term solutions. Tactics are important, but they need to be gelled together within a strategy to gain maximum effectiveness.[3]

So tactics are the detailed decisions that make strategy work. But planned tactics do not create results on their own. Tactics need to be implemented or put into action. The section on 'Action' looks at the real working world of marketing (see page 62).

Strategy is the big picture. Tactics are the details of strategy

How do you implement tactical decisions?

With the situation analysed, objectives quantified, strategies agreed and tactics specified – what is next?

Action. Tactics have to be implemented. This includes project management, schedules and deadlines, meetings and memos, phone calls, chasing people, careful preparation, constant checking and attention to vast volumes of details.

The daily 9–5 of the marketing professional is not all gloss, glimmer and good times generated by suppliers keen to throw wave after wave of Wimbledon and Wembley cup final tickets at fun-frenzied marketing managers. The reality is early starts, traffic jams, bulging in-trays, volumes of research reports, painstaking attention to detail and checking that activities are being carried out correctly. And constant interruptions from your cellular phone. Remember Murphy's Law – what can go wrong will go wrong. Advertisements fall off poster sites, price lists have misprints, products break down, exhibition equipment gets lost in shipping, war breaks out on the day of the new press launch. Random events occur and mistakes happen.

Here's Professor Theodore Levitt, 'Well, we all read about disasters in international marketing, blunders have been committed because of the failure to take notice of the special requirements of special markets and special places. ... but mistakes do get made, everybody makes mistakes, parents make mistakes, police make mistakes, political leaders make mistakes, there's no reason why business people can't also make mistakes, mistakes get made, that's way the world works.'

People make mistakes. And hopefully learn from them. Despite this, the marketing manager not only has to ensure that everything is done correctly at the right time, but by the right person. At the end of the day people implement the tactical details of the marketing mix. New prices have to be circulated, point-of-sale materials have to be fixed in place, shelves have to stacked, exhibitions and conferences have to be rehearsed. Cooperation is crucial. People skills are vital when putting plans into action. Building a team, or simply asking staff to do a job requires people skills and, in particular, communication skills.

Communication skills are needed to get the plan approved by senior management in the first place. Without approval, you have no budget. Without resources you have a useless plan.

Good professionals have contingency plans in case things go wrong. There is no substitute for attention to detail, amidst their hectic daily schedules. So tactics get translated into action. The final stage in the SOSTAC marketing planning process is C for control. The 'Control' section which follows looks at this in more detail.

Everything degenerates into work – strategies and tactics eventually become work that has to be carried out and eventually checked for any mistakes

Do we really need a review?

With the situation analysed, objectives quantified, strategies clarified, tactics put into action, what is next? Control.

Leading, planning, organizing and controlling are core management responsibilities. Plans should have a built-in method of review. This ensures some measure of control. Remember, some forms of control, such as monitoring customer awareness, attitudes, satisfaction and loyalty, cost both time and money. Other forms of control, like sales analysis, cost only time. This should be planned and budgeted for in the marketing plan itself.

Long-term plans can be reviewed once a year, while annual plans are reviewed quarterly or monthly. Monthly plans are reviewed weekly or daily in some cases. If the review identifies a problem at least it can be addressed as opposed to continuing to go unnoticed.

Control systems, or some system of measurement, need to be in place to ensure effective control. Here's how Microsoft build measurement into their control system.

'Measurement and metrics, as they are called these days in the business, are critical. If you have done an effective job of planning, then you should have various business milestones and the absolute things that you are going to measure in place before you ever start to execute your marketing plan. So you might have. Let's look at some of the different ways you could measure business. Revenue is an obvious one: the number of units which you ship, the market share that you are achieving in a particular category. The awareness that people have of your company, these are all very specific measurable activities. The job of the marketer, having decided what the key objectives are, should then determine the measurement and it is very much the responsibility of the marketer to make sure that he has the systems in place that will enable him to track performance in, let's say, market share versus the goals he established as part of the plan.

'In control systems, perhaps we have an advantage of being a software company ourselves. Our control systems are equal to the best in the world. Every morning I can check precisely what our sales were the previous day, the month to date, year to date figures, how it compares with the previous year, the previous quarter, and if you consider that we have no less than 1,000 of what are called

SKUs, stock keeping units (products in other words), to be able to do that at the touch of a button every morning, with data that was last updated at 3 o'clock that previous morning, is a fairly outstanding achievement. That's the sort of thing, in a very competitive market such as the business software industry you need, you have to have that level of finger on the pulse of your activity to make sure that you're absolutely in control of your business.'

So control systems provide an essential loop-back in the marketing planning cycle. The feedback identifies problems and successes that help managers to plan improvements.

So some form of review against specific objectives is a vital control mechanism. This provides feedback that influences future plans. In a sense, planning is a continuous cycle or loop with review/control as the key to an effective planning cycle.

'Control' completes the loop in the SOSTAC marketing planning cycle. Marketing planning then becomes a continuous process of refinement and improvement. The feedback is built into the situation analysis, which affects the objectives (where we want to go). This in turn guides the strategy (how we get there), which in turn drives the tactics (the details of strategy), and then 'everything degenerates into work' or action.

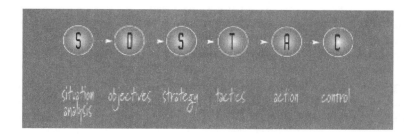

Does SOSTAC work?

For now let's see if marketing managers can actually adopt the SOSTAC approach to their marketing planning process.

David Solomon, TVX, 'It is very interesting actually, because when I look at what we have been doing in the last few months and what we are actually planing to do, it appears that we are following the principles of SOSTAC. Except that if you start with 'S', the situation, we didn't say where are we now, we knew where we were, we were at zero, we had everything to do. So we really were at the stage of the objectives. What are our objectives? Where do we want to go? And where do we feel we can go? In all other respects we would see ourselves very much following from then on the principles of SOSTAC.'

John Leftwick, Microsoft, 'We use something similar to SOSTAC within our own marketing planning. It would depend typically on the scale of the marketing exercise, but certainly, in a full year plan the structure of the document very closely follows the SOSTAC formula. It is an excellent discipline and a way of making sure that you have considered all aspects of your marketing activity, prior to implementing the plan. Equally, while using men, money and minutes, I guess securing the budget from me, is the first standpoint and obviously I have a big say in making sure that it is going to be spent effectively. In working with men, that would involve the sales force; it's then very much on the individual marketing manager's influence and ability as to how well they could influence and direct and get the sales force agreement and commitment to assist him in deployment of the plan. And then the minutes are down to the time-scales through which they are able to implement and deploy their plan.'

Sam Howe, SouthWestern Bell, 'Yes, we have an approach to laying out a marketing plan and it's quite like SOSTAC. In fact, it incorporates key elements of understanding what the situation is: looking in the environment for key indicators; reaching some sort of conclusion about what that means, so people don't have different interpretations about what's happening in the situation; then going on and writing objectives, very specific in timing and degree; strategies that talk broadly about where we're going and then specific tactics. Now I like to follow up tactics, as you have, with SOSTAC –

with specific actions; so a tactic might be, "Let's launch an advertising campaign on this date", but it might action-wise say, "Let direct mail drop in three different waves over these dates". That gets very specific. Now the last thing, that we do somewhat informally but I think SOSTAC really makes concrete, is going back and looking at the control features – how do you know if you're succeeding? How do you know if you need to make some adjustments along the way? That's very critical to making any campaign work, or any marketing initiative at all. When we work on our marketing plans we definitely make trade-offs like the 3Ms. We are always gauging does this take more manpower or does this take more money, how long to develop, everyday you make a trade-off. I will give you an example, we are asking ourselves how often do we have to survey our customers about their perceptions or awareness of our programming. Well we could do a monthly survey but it would cost quite a lot, so we have decided to do a quarterly survey with a bigger sample and get a better statistical read of what's going on in the marketplace. It is more accurate, but it is less frequent, so we traded off some measure of time against money in order to get what we needed.'

So in practice SOSTAC + the 3Ms does actually work.[4]

- Situation analysis (where are we now?)
- Objectives (where do we want to go?)
- Strategy (how are we going to get there)
- Tactics
- Action
- Control
- + 3Ms (men, money and minutes)

SOSTAC – The perfect plan.

Notes

[1]The video browser in Marketing CD ROM Title 2: Segmentation, Positioning and the Marketing Mix (Multimedia Marketing Consortium, London) reveals Kenichi Ohmae talking about time and obsolescence theory, Philip Kotler on time-based competition and Rosabeth Moss Kanter on faster planning cycles.

[2]You can see marketing managers revealing their marketing objectives to the video browser in Marketing CD ROM Title 2: Segmentation, Positioning and the Marketing Mix, Multimedia Marketing Consortium, London.

[3]The video browser in Marketing CD ROM Title 2: Segmentation, Positioning and the Marketing Mix (Multimedia Marketing Consortium, London) shows marketing managers from Microsoft, Southwestern Bell and Concorde Supersonic Jet actually talking about their tactics.

[4]The gurus in the Hall Of Fame in Marketing CD ROM Title 2: Segmentation, Positioning and the Marketing Mix (Multimedia Marketing Consortium, London) answer questions about 500-year plans and the difference between strategy and tactics.

four

buyer
behaviour

- Why do customers buy?
- How are buyers influenced by their situation?
- What are the mental stages of making a purchase?
- What are the major factors that influence buyers?
- What social and cultural factors affect buyers?
- What psychological factors affect buyers?
- How do geodemographics help marketers?
- How are business-to-business markets different to consumer markets?
- What situations affect organizational buyers?
- What stages do industrial, business-to-business and organizational buyers go through when buying?
- What are the hidden influences that affect professional buyers?

Why do customers buy?

Why do customers buy? What goes on inside a customer's mind before, during and after a purchase? How do buyers choose? What are the hidden influences? How do buyers process information? Unlocking these secrets opens the door to success.

Why buy a Coca-Cola? Is it because of thirst? Why buy Levi's jeans? Is it to avoid hypothermia, or to conform to a social norm? Or do some brands offer other benefits... emotional benefits? Are there hidden reasons?

Let's look at the other side. What do the advertisers promise... Coca-Cola will quench your thirst or Levi's will keep your legs warm? Perhaps they appeal to other desires? Look at the advertisements. Try to summarize exactly what you think they are saying. This takes practice. Summarizing advertisements is a skill which top marketing people develop. It may give you an insight into society, its values and aspirations, that is, if you believe that advertising reflects society.

We are not perfectly rational, sensible buyers. We do not always choose goods and services solely on price, performance and availability. The truth is that many purchases are influenced by a whole host of emotional reasons such as esteem and image. Many of these non-rational reasons are hidden deep in our subconscious.[1] In-depth research probes into the dark depths of our unconscious. Some research presents such bizarre explanations that many marketers reject the findings. For example, Ernest Dichter's 1964 handbook of motivations suggested that men buy open-top/convertible cars as substitute mistresses! But even today, top companies use in-depth research techniques to discover the hidden reasons of why we buy or don't buy. Don't forget your own powers of observation. Looking, watching and listening as you travel round the world also provides useful insights into the minds of buyers.[2]

Research helps to find the real reasons of why we buy what we buy. This requires time, money and expertise. Surprisingly, many organizations don't really know exactly why their customers buy or don't buy from them. Yet understanding customers is at the heart of marketing. Once the 'reasons why' people buy, or don't buy, are discovered, the marketing mix can be changed to suit the buyer's needs and wants.

Buyer behaviour involves both simple and complex mental processes. Marketers cannot capture human nature in its entirety, but we can learn a lot about customers through research, observation and thinking. Here's

Professor Theodore Levitt, 'I think it is a process of trying to think your way through why people behave in certain ways… or if not why, why that behaviour is likely to be given certain kinds of products, certain kinds of… just stop to think'.

If men buy soft top sport cars as substitute mistresses,
why do women buy them?

How are buyers influenced by their situation?

A customer's approach to purchasing a product or service is influenced by their situation – whether they have money and how important, frequent, risky or urgent the purchase is to them in their situation.

Imagine the difference between someone with plenty of money, who can afford to make a mistake when buying, as opposed to someone who has scraped his or her last few pounds together. They might both be buying the same product, but their financial situations suggest that their approach to buying is very different.

Customers make more of an effort, and become more involved, if the purchase is relatively important to them, particularly if they have no previous experience of buying such a product or service.

On the other hand, if the item being purchased is low value and frequently bought, like a jar of coffee, it follows that the buyer will spend less time and effort and will have less involvement with the purchase.

These frequent, inexpensive purchases generally have little risk and require less information. These sorts of purchase situations are referred to as 'low involvement purchases'. In these situations, consumers can fall into a routine purchasing pattern that requires little thought and even less effort. Whenever the need is stimulated, a particular brand is automatically purchased. This is called 'routinized response behaviour'.[3]

Alternatively, an expensive high-risk infrequent purchase, such as your first computer, will require a lot of detailed information and careful analysis before deciding on which machine. This is called 'high involvement'. Here the consumer goes through an 'extensive problem-solving' process – searching and collecting information, evaluating it and eventually deciding on a particular choice.

There is a third type of buying situation. This is where the customer has had some experience of buying a particular type of product or service before. There is less risk attached and less information is required. This is called 'limited problem solving'.

Customers require different marketing mixes in different buying situations. For example, a routinized response purchase, like a can of cola, doesn't require much supporting product literature, but perhaps it needs wide distribution and easy availability. An extensive problem-solving type of purchase, on the other hand, would require detailed product literature and trained sales people.

Time also affects the buying situation. If a purchase is urgent, the purchasing pattern will be different from another situation where there is more time available. For example, the decision to call a plumber to a install a new shower is different from calling a plumber to stop a leaking pipe!

To summarize, the three types of consumer buying situation can be put on to a problem-solving continuum.

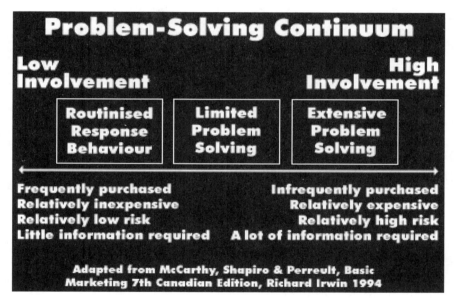

The problem-solving continuum

What are the mental stages of making a purchase?

There are many different models that attempt to map the reality of the buying process. Some are more complex than others.

The problem-solving model below identifies the stages through which a buyer moves: awareness of the need to buy something, is called 'problem recognition'. This is followed by 'information search'. For example, when buying a new multimedia PC, the search could involve: collecting brochures and sales literature, articles and advertisements, visits to shops and exhibitions, talking to sales people, computer experts and friends. The evaluation stage weighs up the criteria, such as size, speed, functions, price, delivery, reliability and guarantee. Eventually a decision is made to choose and buy a particular brand. It doesn't end here as the shop might be out of stock. In this case, the communications mix has worked but the marketing mix has failed – distribution problems exist as the product is not on the shelf where and when it is needed. When eventually a purchase is made, most of us then suffer some anxiety about whether we made the right choice. This worry is called post-purchase dissonance.[4] It is important for marketers to reduce this customer anxiety so that buyers become satisfied customers who develop brand loyalty and become more likely to buy the same brand again if and when the need arises.

The consumer buying process is not always simply a linear process. Customers sometimes loop backwards when, say, they discover a new product function or new criterion which needs to be considered. In addition, not all kinds of purchases require the high involvement problem-solving approach just discussed.

Buying a can of cola, on the other hand, would require less time and effort. It would involve fewer stages in the buying process. It is a simple, low involvement, routine purchase. This 'routinized response behaviour' takes a shortcut by moving from need awareness (problem identification) to memory and straight to choice.

Both of these models hide the detailed workings of the mind. Other models, such as stimulus-response models only show inputs, such as advertising, and outputs, such as sales. Here the complex workings of the mind are ignored and left inside a kind of 'black box'. There are, of course, more complex models which try to open up the black box and look inside the buyer's mind.

There are other simpler communication models such as AIDA, which help marketers to plan their communications.

Although many buying models are criticized, they can provide a loose checklist for a marketing plan.[5] They can also help to give a useful insight into the buying process which is, after all, at the core of marketing.

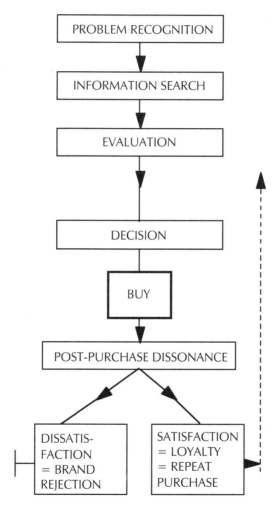

A simple model of the buying process

What are the major factors that influence buyers?

There are many factors that influence the way we behave, and, in particular, the way we buy. These factors can be grouped together into social variables, including cultural, personal characteristics and psychological variables.

All these variables are discussed in more detail in their respective sections. For now, remember that we are all members of some kind of social group. Customers are influenced by the kind of group to which they belong. Social status, family and friends all influence our buying decisions. You can see how some football fans' lifelong buying decisions are determined by their families within hours of their birth in the section on 'What social and cultural factors affect buyers?'

Culture obviously influences what we do and what we buy. Whether it's food or fashion its easy to see how the purchasing habits of, say, an Australian Aborigine is different from that of a New Yorker. Aborigines tend to buy similar types of products as do New Yorkers. And, of course, subcultures influence purchasing patterns, eg New York's Hispanics will have some different purchasing habits than other subcultures within New York.

Personal factors include age, income, job, lifestyle, personality and self-concept. Change any of these factors and see how the purchasing pattern may be affected. Take income and lifestyle – both the buying process and the eventual choice of goods tend to be different if you have a lot of money and a flamboyant lifestyle as opposed to very little money and a quiet lifestyle.

Finally, the psychological variables which influence our buying behaviour. These include: perception, motivation, attitudes and learning. How do we perceive advertisements? What makes us see only a few of the hundreds of advertisements that bombard us each day? How many do we remember and why? What do customers really want? What are their attitudes and how do they learn new ones? How do they learn about new products and new benefits?

Ideally, marketers need to immerse themselves in their customers' minds... becoming totally familiar with their perceptions, their values, their attitudes, their beliefs, the way they learn and, of course, their needs and desires. This knowledge can be used by marketers to influence a customer's buying behaviour.[6]

For now, just remember that marketers must know how social, personal and psychological variables can influence their customers' buying behaviour.

Ask your friends why they buy what they buy and they will almost always try to give you rational reasons as they pretend to be rational animals when in fact there are a host of emotional reasons at play simultaneously.

What social and cultural factors affect buyers?

Customers are influenced by other people. The influence can come from all or any of these social groups:

- Family
- Reference group
- Social class
- Culture and subculture

Family influence is obvious.[7] Some families influence an individual's lifetime buying behaviour within hours of birth; for example, Manchester United football fans register their newly born babies as members of MUFC within hours of the birth!

An individual also looks to his or her reference group when forming an opinion, attitude or belief. The customer may not actually be a member of this group, but may simply aspire to be a member of it and so refer to its value system. The marketer needs to know whether customers are influenced significantly by any reference group and which kind of customer is influenced by which particular reference group. Conspicuous products such as clothes, cars and toys lend themselves to reference group influence. This means that much marketing effort goes into identifying and converting opinion leaders within particular reference groups. Opinion followers then try to follow the leaders by imitating them and sometimes purchasing the same brands.

Social class affects the probability of having children, their chances of survival, their education and much more. It also influences buying behaviour.

Culture and subculture also influence people's lifestyles, beliefs, attitudes and, of course, their buying behaviour. For example, Japanese buy and eat raw fish. Their children learn to like raw fish. However, few European children eat raw fish. Subcultures are pockets of people within a culture who have even greater similarities – they share their own set of values, attitudes and beliefs. They can be formed from national, religious, racial or geographic groups. Colour, dress, music, language, tone of voice, gestures and body language can have different meanings among different cultures and even subcultures. Subcultures not only influence buying patterns, but can also influence the way marketing messages are received.

For example, some research suggests that French-speaking Canadians focus on message source or who is presenting the advertisement, while English-speaking Canadians are more concerned with the content of the advertisement.

The marketer seeks to understand all the group influences that affect customers so that the marketing mix can be adjusted to give the maximum effect.

Families influence an individual's buying behaviour

What psychological factors affect buyers?

The behaviourist school of psychology concentrates on inputs and outputs – stimuli and responses. In marketing this means simply focusing on whether people respond to stimuli, like advertisements or mail shots by, say, making a purchase. Behavioural psychology ignores the complex mechanisms of the mind by dumping all the psychological variables into a 'black box'.

Cognitive psychology, on the other hand, tries to open the lid and look inside the black box by delving into the complexities of the human mind. Buying behaviour is, in fact, affected by a complex web of internal psychological variables. These include perception, motivation, learning, memory, attitudes and personality.

Perception, in marketing terms, means how commercial stimuli like advertisements are seen, interpreted and remembered. Customers tend to engage in 'selective perception' – they see what they want to see. They also sometimes distort some messages to fit their view of the world. Screening out unpleasant messages and non-relevant messages allows buyers to engage in 'selective retention'. Given that perception is influenced by motivation, it is worth while researching what exactly motivates and stimulates customers. Imagine sending a message that demotivated, or worse, irritated your target market? Just as good advertising may increase sales, bad advertising can decrease sales. Understanding how customers see themselves, their self-image or self-concept, is important, as many goods and services are chosen because they reinforce the buyers self-concept. For example, packaging should reflect and not conflict with the customer's ideal self-image.

What makes a customer want a particular image? What are a customer's underlying motivations? A motive is a drive to satisfy a need. Maslow's hierarchy of needs (see below) provides a useful theory that, when slightly simplified, suggests that we are motivated to satisfy a higher level of need once we have satisfied a lower level need. Sigmund Freud suggested that we are motivated by conscious and unconscious forces.

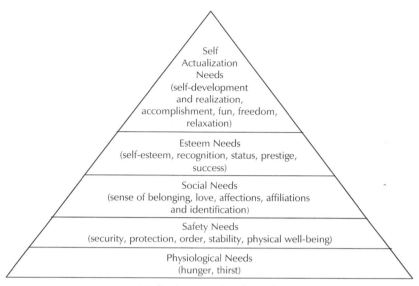

Maslow's Hierarchy of Needs

Motivation, in turn, affects perception and learning. How do consumers learn and remember marketing messages? How many advertisements does each customer need to see? When does the advertising become both a waste of money and an irritant? Add attitudes and personalities to the other complexities of the mind and you can see that these questions are difficult to answer precisely.

Although it requires skill, time and money, getting inside the customer's mind is essential and unavoidable in the quest for continuous marketing success... and it can lead to exciting discoveries (eg some Guinness drinkers believe Guinness has Celtic mystical powers).

Getting inside your customer's mind is essential

How do geodemographics help marketers?

Customer behaviour is influenced by a host of personal factors, many of which can be categorized under demographics. This includes age, sex, race, ethnic origin, income, job, family and stage of family life cycle. There are many products and services that are bought only for users who fall into one specific demographic category. Take the family life cycle. A newly married couple will be more interested in furniture and utensils than retirement holidays. A couple with a new baby will obviously be interested in baby products, while parents with teenage children will not. And so on through the family life cycle. Therefore marketers can target customers that fall within a certain stage of the family life cycle.

Marketers are also interested in other personal factors, such as where customers live.

Geodemographics combines geographic and demographic data together to find clusters of demographic groups within certain geographical areas. This can provide the marketer with valuable information about the target market. Since the 1980s, geodemographic databases have become a major marketing tool for many consumer marketers. For example, they have been targeting 'prosperous pensioners in retirement areas, affluent greys in rural communities and better off executives in inner city areas'.

Marketing managers are generally interested in the aggregate numbers rather than one-off individual exceptions. They are usually interested in the trend... is there a concentration or cluster of similar customers in the market?

Whether demographics, geodemographics or plain common sense is used, the marketer must know as much as possible about target customers, what they want, where they live, how they buy, when they buy, how much they can spend, what their values are, and much more. This is important, as personal factors influence buyer behaviour both directly and indirectly.

'You are where you live.' Gedoemographic clustering can predict your likelihood to purchase certain brands, once you reveal your post code

How are business-to-business markets different to consumer markets?

Organizational markets are 'business-to-business' markets where the buyers buy on behalf of their business or organization. They may be buying tons of chemicals, new computer systems or just office envelopes.

Organizational markets include industrial organizations such as car manufacturers or institutions like hospitals; resellers such as wholesalers or retail stores; and vast numbers of bodies such as local government and central government.

These markets are different from consumer markets in many ways. There are generally fewer buyers, but they place bigger orders. This is because industrial demand is often derived from the primary demand generated in consumer markets.

Organizational buyers forge close relationships with their suppliers by developing strategic alliances, partnership sourcing, and organizational mating. This basically means that today buyers and suppliers work much closer together than in the old days of adversarial marketing.

Organizational buyers may be concentrated geographically in industrial towns, cities and trading estates, while the suppliers can be spread out across the international horizon. Global suppliers travel in search of new buyers continually. Many major buyers simultaneously 'out source globally' – that is they source their supplies from all over the global economy.[8]

Organizational buyers are said to be much more rational than consumer buyers. This is not always the case. It can depend on the type of individual and type of organization.[9]

There may be more than one person involved in the decision to buy or not to buy. Compared to consumers, organizational buyers tend to have at least one extra member in the decision-making unit... and that is the gatekeeper – sometimes a secretary or PA whose job it is to protect the boss from unwanted interruptions from uninvited salespeople.

Many organizational markets have a policy of only buying from a previously approved 'preferred supplier' or 'listed' supplier. In this case, the marketers first priority is simply to get 'listed' or approved.

Finally, industrial marketing managers tend to spend a greater proportion of their budgets on their sales force than on advertising. This contrasts with consumer markets, where it tends to be the other way around. This is, however, changing as many commercial products are now appearing on domestic television, for example, photocopiers.

Organizational markets are different from consumer markets. They generally involve bigger purchases, more rational choices, more formal decision-making units or purchasing policies and closer supplier relationships, which may be spread globally. Despite the differences, the principle is the same – stick close to customers and their needs.

Business customers are different from domestic customers

What situations affect organizational buyers?

An organization's approach to buying is influenced by its situation: how much money it can afford; the size and risk of the purchase as well as the actual buying situation; whether it is a new task, a modified rebuy or straight rebuy.

A 'new task' buying situation means what it says – the organization is embarking on a new task for the first time of buying a particular product or service.

A 'modified rebuy' situation is where the industrial buyer has some experience of the product or service, while a 'straight rebuy' is where the buyer or purchasing department buys a particular product or service regularly. Here, the buyer reorders on a routine basis from a list of approved or preferred suppliers.

Some sales people are better in certain buying situations than others. Some 'order getters' typically revel in the challenge of winning new business, and other sales people, 'order takers', prefer to service existing customers who need to reorder regularly – a straight rebuy situation.

Time also affects the buying situation. Consider an emergency purchase. Imagine a manufacturer's stock of raw materials is damaged by a fire or its supplier suddenly goes into liquidation. The time available for sourcing new suppliers is limited. And the time available for delivery is even shorter. Although more costly, a quicker purchase, which means a shorter selection process, may in this situation be necessary to keep the factory going. Incidentally, this is where marketing intelligence is important to the sales representative. If the representative knows that the buyer is desperate to buy, then terms can be dictated to get a better deal.

But remember, exploiting a customer in a one-off sale is a dangerous type of short-term marketing. Excellent marketing looks to the longer term, to build good customer relations on trust and fair dealing so that repeat business can blossom through a relationship marketing approach.

Finally, a buyer's level of involvement or effort, the number of people involved in the decision and the length and rigour of the decision-making process will be influenced by the size and risk of the purchase as well as the particular type of buying situation – new task, modified rebuy or straight rebuy. The section on the buying process (on page 88) looks at the actual buying process in more detail.

New task, modified rebuy or straight rebuy?

What stages do industrial, business-to-business and organizational buyers go through when buying?

Organizational buying can be a rigorous process, particularly if the purchase is sufficiently large and risky enough to require a high level of effort and involvement.

Let's look at a major 'new task' purchase and see how the whole buying process is slowly and carefully carried out.

Starting with problem recognition, the organization acknowledges that it needs to buy a product or service. The need is then carefully defined and eventually a detailed product specification is drawn up.

Potential suppliers may be invited to present their credentials before being invited to tender a proposal. From a supplier's perspective, getting on to a list of 'preferred suppliers' or tender list is vital. If you're not on either the tender list or the preferred suppliers list you're excluded from even trying to sell. This is now the general rule for buying organizations from the Paris Town Hall to the Pentagon.

After careful analysis, and sometimes further negotiations, a supplier is selected and a purchase order is placed with a particular supplier.

Incidentally, some organizations' buying policies insist on buying from more than a single supplier in case anything goes wrong with one of the suppliers. You can see why many organizations today prefer to forge close relations with their suppliers so that they don't have to go through a costly, time-consuming and rigorous process every time they buy.

In ongoing purchase situations such as a 'straight rebuy' or 'modified rebuy', major suppliers are reviewed regularly as part of total quality management (TQM).

This means agreeing a performance review, cooperating, sharing information and striving to improve both parties' performances. Strategic partnerships, strategic alliances, organizational mating and partnership sourcing are terms which indicate the importance of the close working relationship between buyers and suppliers in organizational markets.

Finally, the buyer's situation and purchasing policies influence the buying process. For example, a 'straight rebuy' for a low-value item will have a shorter buying process than a major 'new task' purchase. Equally, a purchasing policy may require purchases over a certain value to have a minimum of three quotations from three different suppliers. There may also be a minimum quality standard where only suppliers who have attained a specific standard of quality are allowed to offer their goods and services.

Understanding the buying process helps the marketing manager to win and keep customers by moving them carefully through each stage of their particular buying process.

Understanding the buying process helps to keep customers by moving them carefully through each stage of their buying process

What are the hidden influences that affect professional buyers?

In organizational markets buyers are influenced directly and indirectly by at least four categories of factors:

- the business environment;
- organization structure;
- interpersonal relationships;
- individual buyer characteristics.

The business environment includes the uncontrollable external factors such as economics, politics, technology and business, and social issues such as ethics.

A buyer's decision is also influenced by an organization's culture and structure of committees and decision-making units, along with formal and/or centralized buying procedures.

Then there are the interpersonal factors within the decision-making unit. These involve authority, status, role and group dynamics. Many have the power to say 'no', but few have the power to say 'yes' when making a buying decision. Ultimately, the senior buyer has a lot of power and status.

The characteristics of individual buyers obviously affect the ultimate buying behaviour. Buyers vary according to the stage in their careers, their age, ambition, ego and ability. Some are risk averse and some are risk seekers. Some will buy an innovative idea, others will run away from it.

Personality and personal relationships can play a key part in organizational buying behaviour.

To summarize, there are many factors which can affect an organization's buying behaviour. The economy, an organization's structure, the buyer's power base, the buyer's personality and personal relationships are all factors of influence in organizational buying behaviour.[10]

Are there hidden influences that affect organizational buyers?

Notes

[1]You can see SouthWestern Bell and Microsoft talking about this supposed 'emotional/rational dichotomy' in the video browser in Marketing CD ROM Title 4: Buying Behaviour, Multimedia Marketing Consortium, London.

[2]Japan's Kenichi Ohmae explains in the browser in Marketing CD ROM Title 4: Buying Behaviour (Multimedia Marketing Consortium, London) why he sits for hours in shopping malls watching customers.

[3]You can visit the Hall of Fame in Marketing CD ROM Title 4: Buying Behaviour (Multimedia Marketing Consortium, London) later to see the gurus explain how brands influence routine purchases.

[4]You can see Professor Peter Doyle talking about Cognitive Dissonance in the video browser in Marketing CD ROM Title 4: Buying Behaviour, Multimedia Marketing Consortium, London.

[5]Models can be criticized, for instance see Professor Doyle in the browser in Marketing CD ROM Title 4: Buying Behaviour, Multimedia Marketing Consortium, London.

[6]Later, in the browser Marketing CD ROM Title 4: Buying Behaviour (Multimedia Marketing Consortium, London), you can see how football fans really desire, and buy, transcendence. You can also see Ted Levitt explaining how marketing influences our basic needs.

[7]Later, in Marketing CD ROM Title 4: Buying Behaviour (Multimedia Marketing Consortium, London), video browser, you can see how football fans really desire, and buy, transcendence. You can also see Ted Levitt explaining how our basic needs are influenced by marketing.

[8]You can see Kenichi Ohmae in the video browser talking about the borderless world in Marketing CD ROM Title 4: Buying Behaviour, Multimedia Marketing Consortium, London.

[9]You can hear Professor Peter Doyle talking about the emotional/rational dichotomy of industrial markets in the video browser Marketing CD ROM Title 4: Buying Behaviour, Multimedia Marketing Consortium, London.

[10]In Marketing CD ROM Title 4: Buying Behaviour (Multimedia Marketing Consortium, London), you can find at the end of the Picture Browser some text examples showing how some strong relationships between buyers and sellers ensure that certain suppliers never win their business.

marketing
research

- ➔ Do we really need to collect more information?
- ➔ What is a marketing information system?
- ➔ What kinds of market research can help?
- ➔ How do you manage a market research project?
- ➔ What internal sources provide valuable information?
- ➔ Why pay £10,000 when £1 will do?
- ➔ What is qualitative research?
- ➔ What is quantitative research?
- ➔ Can you give me an example of marketing research in a consumer market?
- ➔ Can you give me an example of marketing research in an organizational/business-to-business or industrial situation?
- ➔ How will the IT explosion affect marketing research?
- ➔ What is low-tech common sense?

Do we really need to collect more information?

One of these cards is an ace. Can you pick it? You know it's there, but can you select it? Are you sure?

Many business decisions have elements of uncertainty and risk attached to them. Choices have to be made. Most decisions have some kind of risk attached to them.

But how can you reduce risk? What would help you to reduce risk and make the correct choice? Can you identify the ace yet?

So perhaps you would prefer to choose the ace now? Almost certainly you feel you now have a better chance of success.

So what has happened here? Information reduces the risk. In fact, knowing three of the cards reduces the risk to zero.

Wouldn't life be great if you could get perfect information like this all the time! All our marketing decisions would be zero risk – guaranteed to succeed. Always knowing the correct answers to questions like 'How much advertising should I do? What should I say? What should I call my product? When should I advertise? Where should I advertise? How often? What price should I charge? What product should I make? How often should I deliver? Which customers are best? Where are they? How do I contact them?'

Knowing what you need to know is vital. Specifying precisely what information you need is the first step. Ask the wrong questions and you get the wrong answers. Then you drown in a sea of useless information.

So wrong questions cost time and money. Wrong questions and irrelevant information generate confusion, chaos and ultimately misinformed decisions – the seeds of failure. The seeds of success, however, lie in the ability to ask the right questions, to know what you need to find out. Before making decisions you need to decide what information is needed to make a particular decision. Then, can you realistically get the information? How long will it take? How much will it cost? Can you afford it? Is it worth it or is some information more important than other information?

And finally, information used in the right way is a powerful marketing tool. Accurate, relevant information can create competitive advantage. It helps marketers to make better decisions. The corollary is also true: inaccurate, irrelevant information is dangerous.

So information reduces risk but costs time and money. Consider, firstly, whether the information is worth more than it costs and, secondly, how important are the decisions which it will affect?

The ability to asking the right question is a much sought after skill

What is a marketing information system?

A marketing information system is basically a way of regularly gathering and giving helpful marketing information to the right people at the right time.

The key element is knowing what kind of information is needed, by whom and when. Information needs, information sources and information costs change over time and so a review, or information audit, is worth doing every few years. An information audit specifies who needs what and when. The audit can also list where the information can be found – the gold mine of information sources. There are many different types of information that a marketing manager uses, and many ways of building a marketing information system. Here is one way of thinking about it. Consider these components:

- Internal information
- External information
- Position information
- Decision information
- Forecast information

Examples of internal information are sales reports, sales analyses, cost per sale and cost per enquiry. Most of the raw data is already available within the organization. It just needs to be processed or analysed so that it becomes helpful information. This is relatively easy to do if there is an information system. Customer database systems, for example, automatically convert customer data into marketing opportunities such as identifying which customers are ready to buy this month, next month or next year.

External information covers the market out there – its size, structure, trends, opportunities, threats, competitors and customers both new and old – the constantly changing marketplace. All kinds of employees, customers and distributors can contribute to this pool of marketing intelligence.

Position information puts internal and external information together, like the organization's sales and the overall sales in the market to calculate market share. Similarly, internal strengths and weaknesses can be compared to competitors to find competitive advantage, USPs (unique selling points), and most importantly whether any competitive advantage is sustainable.

Decision information comes from mathematical models, which carry out various analyses such as regression, correlation, factor and cluster analyses.[1]

Forecast information obviously looks into the future and includes sales forecasts – the backbone of the marketing plan.

Some of this information is free, some is expensive, some takes time to gather and analyse, some is just not worth the effort in the first place.

There is, therefore, a trade-off between the importance or value of information and its cost – in terms of time and money. Experienced managers know which information affects which decisions. They know which information is vital. Do you?

Amidst a sea of 'too much information' managers must think carefully about exactly what information they require

What kinds of market research can help?

There are some general categories of research – primary and secondary; qualitative and quantitative. Primary research is carried out primarily for an organization's own use. Secondary research uses research already carried out by someone else for some other purpose. Desk research checks secondary sources before carrying out the more expensive primary research.

Qualitative research delivers soft data which reveals *why* buyers buy or *why* they remember. Quantitative research delivers hard data – such as numbers and percentages of buyers who buy, or who remember advertisements.

Research can basically provide information on almost anything from markets to competitors to distributors to customers, their behaviour, their attitudes, their intentions and more.

Market reports provide information on markets, their size, structure, key players, their market share, trends, prices and more. These reports are published annually and are available as secondary sources.

Retail audits measure market sales, competitors' sales, market share, prices, special offers and stock levels week by week or day by day.

Customer surveys use carefully structured questionnaires to measure customer attitudes, levels of awareness, intentions to purchase, actual purchases and much more.

Qualitative research techniques, such as focus groups and in-depth interviews, can reveal deeper customer thoughts, motivations, perceptions and reactions to old and new products, packs, prices or advertisements.

Customer reactions can also be measured by simulated test markets and, ultimately, real test markets.

Consumer panels provide information on customer lifestyles, media habits and consumption patterns, while insights into future customer lifestyles are forecast by social forecasters and futurologists.

Research is available for almost any type of information required. But remember – always start with desk research – think secondary first – always see if someone else has already done the work for you. Mind you, you need to look carefully at the relevance and accuracy of other people's information before using it to make your own decisions.

Finally, check why you need the information in the first place. Ask what decisions it will affect?

This helps to screen out the less important information which can drown a busy manager. After that you can choose what type of marketing research best suits your information needs.

Before acquiring information ask, 'Why am I collecting this information? How will I use it? What decision will it affect?

How do you manage a market research project?

There is a sequence of activities, a process, involved in marketing research.

First, define the precise information required, then plan the research, collect the data, analyse it, present the findings and, finally, use the information to make better decisions.

The first stage involves clearly defining the problem or the specific information needed. This is crucial. What information do you need? How will it affect your decisions?

The next stage is to develop a research plan. This means planning how to collect, store and analyse the information, how long it will take to get it, and how much it will cost. Decisions about research methods and sources, whether secondary or primary, qualitative or quantitative, need detailed consideration. The selection of research tools, sample types and sizes all need to be carefully planned. Some plans build in piloting or testing the research to see if it works.

Sometimes several research agencies are invited to make research proposals showing how they plan to collect the required information within the specified timescale and budget.

After the detailed planning comes the execution – collecting the data – whether by survey, discussion group or other method.

Next comes the analysis. In the case of quantitative research this means crunching the numbers; and in the case of qualitative research this means interpreting the discussions, drawings and suggestions.

Next comes the presentation – the research is written up in a report and the key findings are presented along with the research structure and the detailed calculations. The good researcher will also provide implications/recommendations, even if the client subsequently decides to ignore the advice!

Last, but certainly not least, comes the interesting bit – the reason why the research was carried out in the first place... to help to make a decision. Using the information means taking guidance from the research to make a better marketing decision.

Marketing research doesn't make decisions, it simply helps managers to make better decisions – more informed decisions.

Successful decisions are helped by good information. The quality of the information is directly affected by the quality of the whole research process. It needs to be managed carefully.

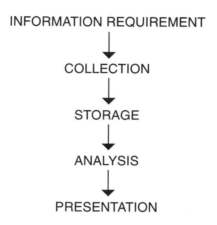

INFORMATION REQUIREMENT

↓

COLLECTION

↓

STORAGE

↓

ANALYSIS

↓

PRESENTATION

The marketing research process

What internal sources provide valuable information?

There is a wealth of marketing information within an organization.

The accounting department, personnel and even customer care departments collect data primarily for their own use. Some of this data should automatically flow into the marketing information system as it can provide a useful secondary source of information for the marketing manager.

The accounting department collects a lot of data about sales, costs and contribution or profitability per product. Sales and marketing managers need to have this kind of information at their fingertips.

Many marketing managers like to have access to yearly, quarterly, monthly, weekly and even daily updated sales figures. Here's Microsoft Marketing Director, John Leftwich.

> 'Every morning I can check precisely what our sales were the previous day, the month to date, year to date figures, how it compares with the previous year, the previous quarter, and if you consider that we have no less than 1000 of what are called SKUs (stock keeping units), products in other words, to be able to do that at the touch of a button every morning with data that was last updated at just 3 o'clock that previous morning, is a fairly outstanding achievement. In addition to sales figures, marketers are also interested in cost figures so that cost per sales, cost per order and cost per enquiry calculations can give an indication of the efficiency of the marketing effort. The raw data is often collected by accountants for other purposes. This raw data is available within all organizations – all it takes is a system which automatically collects, analyses and communicates these figures regularly to the marketing manager. Sales force reports also provide the marketing manager with a rich source of information. Reports can list reasons why business is being won or lost, what customers are saying, what competitors are up to and what's generally happening in the marketplace.'

Other secondary internal sources of information include customer complaint tapes, customer feedback forms and customer letters. Sometimes personnel, customer care or PR departments may collect this information for their own purposes. Some marketing managers keep in touch by listening to taped customer complaints while driving in their cars.

Press clippings showing favourable and unfavourable press coverage are kept by PR departments. They sometimes calculate scores according to the quantity and quality of the press coverage. Again, this kind of information can be useful to a marketing manager, particularly if the press are saying exactly the opposite to what a proposed new advertising campaign is about to say!

There are many internal sources of information that can provide low-cost valuable information – if the marketing information system is in place to collect, store, retrieve and use the information in the first place.

There are many internal sources which provide a goldmine of information

Why pay £10,000 when £1 will do?

All marketing decisions should be based on solid information. Expensive primary research should only be used when all possible secondary sources have been checked.

Why pay many thousands of pounds for a customized market research report when it may be possible to pay a lot less for a shared market research report? These reports, or syndicated surveys, are commissioned by a group of companies in a particular industry sector and can deliver a comprehensive market report only to the commissioning group of companies.

Alternatively, some markets are regularly researched by independent market research companies who sell their research reports to anyone for a few hundred pounds.

Academic researchers also publish research findings on various aspects of the marketing process, often within specific industry sectors at an even lower cost.

Government departments collect, analyse and publish a vast array of facts, figures, surveys and reports.

Newspapers, trade journals and trade associations regularly publish surveys and market reports for as little as the cover price. Why pay £10,000 when £1 might do?

The burden of scanning the press, wandering through libraries and searching among mountains of journals can be reduced with database search facilities.

Both CD ROM databases and on-line databases can search journals, newspapers and magazines for key words. Some databases cover books, research reports and dissertations. Other on-line services such as news groups on the Internet are a great source of marketing intelligence.

A sound marketing information system logs all secondary sources, including libraries and individual writers, contact names, phone numbers and dates of publication. Remember – librarians, archivists, journalists and authors are usually helpful with desk research.

Think secondary first!

Secondary sources are cheaper and faster – whether it's a complete market report or just a key fact, figure or name. But remember, the accuracy and reliability of the secondary source must also be considered.

So to summarize: define your information needs; think secondary first; and exercise caution with all secondary sources.

Why waste money on expensive primary research if it's already available through far cheaper secondary sources?

What is qualitative research?

Primary research is gathered specifically for an organization's own particular use. Competitors cannot get it. Secondary research, on the other hand, has been gathered by someone else for some other purpose – for example, government reports or newspaper features.

There are essentially two types of primary research: qualitative and quantitative.

Quantitative methods provide estimates of how many people buy various items, statistics on who reads certain newspapers, percentages that recall various advertisements, the balance of opinion among a given target group. Quantitative research delivers hard data such as numbers.

Qualitative research, like focus group discussions, ignores hard numbers and provides soft data about people's views, feelings, thoughts and behaviour. It explains, in the customers' own words, why they buy or don't buy, why they like or don't like a new product, pack or advertisement. It can unearth the real reason which is often hidden below the surface.

Qualitative research can be used as exploratory – to search for the issues to be included in the bigger quantitative survey. Qualitative research can also be 'explanatory' – to explain a quantitative survey's findings such as, 'Why older men buy brand X and younger men buy brand Y'.

Qualitative research is usually not statistically reliable because it is not statistically representative – it usually involves only small numbers of respondents in detailed discussions.

Unlike the tightly structured questions used in a large-scale quantitative survey, qualitative research uses relatively unstructured and informal discussions with a small number of respondents sometimes on a one-to-one basis, called 'in-depth interviews', and at other times with a small group of six to eight people, called a 'focus group'.

The interview, or discussion, is generally led by an executive who fully understands the purpose of the research. Discussions can have an observer, be watched through a two-way mirror or be recorded on video. Visual cues, such as body language, are taken into account in the interpretation. That's why many marketing managers watch the actual interviews as well as read the focus group reports.

There are several other less widely used techniques in qualitative research, such as sentence completion, word association, role playing, clay modelling and more. These throw the respondent's ego off-guard and allow the inner, deeper feelings to be expressed.

Although qualitative research provides crucial insights, it does not generally provide statistically valid conclusions.

> Focus groups are to serious research what bumper stickers are to philosophy.

– those that say this are a little harsh, as focus groups can reveal crucial insights which can be subsequently substantiated with quantitative research.

What is quantitative research?

Quantitative methods provide hard data – that means numbers and percentages of types of buyers, types of audiences and much more.

For example, quantitative surveys can count the number and type of people that are aware of a particular brand, aware of its advantages or disadvantages, prefer it or dislike it, buy it or even intend to buy it.

And all of these can be measured before, during and after a particular marketing campaign to see, for example, if an advertising campaign is working.

These quantitative techniques involve structured interviews with large numbers of respondents.

Tightly structured questionnaires are used to ensure that every respondent is asked exactly the same questions and that the answers are recorded in exactly the same way.

Several hundred and sometimes thousands of respondents are chosen as samples to represent a specific market.

Sample selection is a key part of any primary research project. Those samples are statistically representative of the relevant target group. The most expensive approach is a randomly preselected sample of respondents. Several attempts will be made to get an interview with the chosen named respondents – wherever they happen to live. A cost-effective alternative is a quota sample, where the interviewer must complete interviews with consumers from a certain type or quota of age groups, occupations, and so on. A quota defines the profile of the required respondents, for example, 'mothers of children aged between 4 and 12 who buy prerecorded videos'.

The raw data, or respondents' answers, can be collected by phone, mail, street interviews, door-to-door interviews and hall tests.

There are lots of potential pitfalls with research. Managers have to watch for problems which can jeopardize the validity of the research findings.[2]

Remember 'qualitative before quantitative'. Consider whether qualitative research can identify any issues that should be included in the quantitative work. And 'think secondary first'. Check to see if anyone else has carried out the research already. Finally, define your information requirements carefully. Keep asking, 'What information do I need?'

*Before commissioning your own primary research, check
whether the research has been already carried out by someone else*

Can you give me an example of marketing research in a consumer market?

Marketing managers cannot survive without a constant pipeline of relevant information. They need to know about emerging issues, shifts in customer perceptions, how likely they are to buy, why certain customers buy or don't buy, what advertisements are getting through and much more.

Marketers generally draw on a mix of research tools using primary and secondary sources, qualitative and quantitative techniques.

Here's Sam Howe from SouthWestern Bell on how they use marketing research and marketing information systems.

'We carry out all kinds of market research to know more about our customers. It probably falls into two or three types. One is trend kind of analysis where every year we do almost the same piece of research to see how we are changing. For instance, how is the customer perceiving the channels we offer, do they still see one particular channel that's arts and performance, let's say, the same way they did last year, or has something changed? That's one piece of research. Another would be one-offs, if you will, where we want to explore a particular issue. For instance, in the north west of England we have one community that's taking up cable television at a much slower rate than another. Well, we can conjecture why that might be, but on the other hand it might be a good idea, and which we have done, gone in and just look to respondents in that community to tell us what it is about you or your community that has been a problem.

'In addition to those other kinds of market research, we also will tend to look at research that gets at the barriers. Why do people not buy our product? We can't always know that from trend analysis or, let's say, from even one-offs. Periodically we will ask customers who are not our customers 'why aren't you with us?' and we will go in and do specific research, testing particular issues, maybe it's a benefit statement that they are not hearing, or maybe it's a certain attribute of the product we're not aware of that they are focusing on.

'Here's how we know if we are doing well or not in our marketing. We have our standard reports – the numbers, if you will, week on, month on – you know, have we grown? That's easy, but we also have some key measures we look for, that really are to relate back to our strategies. Let's say we want to improve customer awareness of a particular product; well, we can measure likelihood to buy – has that moved up? Awareness of products: simply asking you 'Are you aware of Discovery Channel?' – a little bit more this month or a little bit less; why is that? We can always check then if we are doing the right things to move people along.

'Now, beyond all that, we also can do one-off pieces of research, to say 'We're not sure if we're doing well here or not; let's go in and ask' – that's a quick way to find out. The last thing is simple focus groups – if you want a quick, easy measure, not necessarily one you want to go and do something about immediately but at least to get a gut feel, that's a good way to go.'

Marketers generally draw on a mix of research tools using primary and secondary sources, and qualitative and quantitative techniques in order to reduce risk in decision making.

Can you give me an example of marketing research in an organizational/business-to-business or industrial situation?

Organizational marketing research is fundamentally the same as consumer marketing research. Both use primary and secondary sources, qualitative and quantitative techniques, internal and external sources.

Both use telephone interviews, face-to-face interviews, but organizational marketing research does not use street surveys, door-to-door interviews or hall tests.

Take Concorde supersonic jets – their customers are mostly corporate or business people from major corporations. They use marketing research all the time. Face-to-face interviews, customer surveys and even internal accounting provide a constant supply of vital marketing information. Here is Concorde's marketing manager, Peter Liney.

'Researching Concorde passengers actually isn't too bad. The primary place that we do it is in the lounge. People tend to turn up for Concorde approximately 40 minutes to an hour before we actually depart. They are there in the lounge and now some of those are making last minute telephone calls, but many of them aren't and they are very happy to talk to us about the aircraft. We also will research them on board, that has to be done very discreetly, and this can obviously only be done if they are happy to be spoken to. But what you find is that the frequent Concorde passenger isn't buying this service *per se*, so they are not interested in the meal, and so there, if you like, if they are not working they may not be happy to talk to you on board. So primarily we do it either in the lounge or on board.

'Historically, we try to do it at their work place and as they are quite frankly such senior individuals it can be quite difficult to get time in their diaries.

'As a manager in terms of reviewing the performance of Concorde, I would look to two primary things to tell me whether or not if I'm doing well.

'The first is customer satisfaction. We have ongoing measures of whether or not our customers are saying this is good or bad. Not only in terms of market research, which we would conduct periodically, but we have the customer complaints and so on a monthly basis I know how many people have written in to complain about Concorde or have phoned to complain about it and what they have complained about. So I can very quickly get a handle on do we have any issues that are growing here that are outside of the norm.

'The second area there again on control is I know what the financial performance is. So again I can quickly get a view on how we're doing this month and what the forward bookings are like. So how many people have booked now for December and how does that compare with last year? Is it up? Is it down? If it's down, is it down by a lot? If it's down by a lot, do we have to put some incentive in now in order to get those bookings up? So the two things that I would be looking at are the weekly sales figures, weekly forward bookings and the performance in terms of customer complaints and then on a longer scale the overall customer satisfaction studies we would conduct either annually or biannually.'

So there you have some of the marketing research tools which BA use to help them to market their supersonic jets.

> Marketing research reduces risk and aids decision making. It doesn't replace decision making.

How will the IT explosion affect marketing research?

Information can create competitive advantage. Agile marketers must keep abreast with the relentless pace of change in information technology. From digitization, to scanners, to databases to on-line interactivity – the IT explosion is here. Here are a few additional thoughts from world gurus.

Professor Ted Levitt, 'You know the digitalization of everything involves really constantly the instant conversion of an action into a piece of data that's easily accessible all over the world, instantly, like the speed of light – as a matter of fact that's 137,000 miles a second I believe, or some number, some multiple thereof; I don't recall my elementary physics. The digitalization of everything is a powerful influence on everything. And that means that information more rapidly created, more rapidly transmitted, more rapidly massaged. So that data can be converted into information, it becomes more powerful as a competitive device'.

Professor Peter Doyle, 'New technology is going to have a major impact on market research. I think the principles are going to be valid. The basic principles of understanding your customer, trying to find out what makes him or her tick and using this, those principles will apply. But technology is going to produce change. For example, scanning technology in supermarkets is going to give manufacturers much more information about how customers make decisions. More and more companies, too, are building up databanks which they can access with computers and to give us much more accurate information about their customers, so a grasp at technology, an access to technology will give modern companies a competitive advantage in tomorrow's markets. Technology is going to have a big impact and all of us need to make sure we are at the forefront of this'.

Professor Rosabeth Moss Kanter, 'I think we will use computer interactivity, to have customers tell us on-line as they use a product how they like it, what's good about it, how they'd modify it, and the marketing department is going to have to be even closer to customers in terms of interacting with customers. And the marketing department might also be the translator of those elements of feedback from the customer, translate very quickly what they're hearing from the customer right into the product design process. So within a matter of days or weeks there's the new product that embodies those preferences. So the ability for marketing to be more agile, faster moving and to use new technology is going to grow'.

So whether you're surfing the net or playing with your calculator, IT is now an inseparable ingredient of marketing practice.

The IT explosion permeates almost every aspect of marketing

What is low-tech common sense?

Marketing research, and marketing itself, has scientific elements, statistical analyses and many sophisticated high-tech aids that help marketers to make better decisions, but basic common sense should never be abandoned.

You don't have to be a feedback fanatic. Managers often make decisions based on intuition and experience. Sometimes, the level of risk involved just doesn't justify the time or money required to carry out further research. On top of this, research sometimes gets it wrong, particularly with new products and new ideas – as people find it hard to imagine them in reality. Fax machines and VCRs got negative research, while the doomed New Coke got positive feedback.[3]

As a marketer you must keep your common sense. You must also develop and maintain your ability to understand and stay close to the customer, to watch and observe people, to talk to customers and colleagues, to ask key questions, to seek improvements and to think for yourself.

We all have these abilities, but do we have the discipline to use them? Do we have the time? Do we have the confidence to make the time to do these things – to sit back and think instead of rushing around like headless chickens! Here are some expert thoughts about common sense.

> Harvard's Professor Rosabeth Moss Kanter suggests 'That there are certain research functions – marketing research functions – that are sometimes provided by outside firms that are specialists in doing nothing but research. But the core aspect of marketing, which is understanding our customer and having a close bond with the customer, that should never be turned over to anybody else'.

> Japan's Kenichi Ohmae says 'All I can see is that I constantly travel around the world and I personally stay in touch. When I go to a new city I put on the sneakers and jeans and sit at the supermarket or plaza where the trading activities take place and watch people, what they do, what kind of things they are buying, how much patience they have in queuing up, etc, how fat they are, how not fat they are, etc, what they are wearing, and in each market that I travel through, I do this. Sometimes, as I said, I talked to one or two persons in depth, why I spent days with the users of the product, and then something will come into my mind. The single most important quality is the inquisitive mind. A person will have to ask questions.

'You know people ask if the customers are satisfied, but the real honest question is are we really satisfied, and that if we were the customer what we are offering is really an ideal product or services and it takes a very inquisitive mind, and a good marketing company tends to have this inquisitive mind. It is not impolite to ask questions even to the president, that are we really selling the right product?'

An inquisitive mind, common sense observation and good use of research mean industrial espionage is not required

❝You should take responsibility for informing yourself, and being knowledgeable.❞

Professor Theodore Levitt

Notes

[1]You can see Coca-Cola talking about decision models in the video browser in Marketing CD ROM Title 5: Marketing Research, Multimedia Marketing Consortium, London.

[2]You can see later in the browser in Marketing CD ROM Title 5: Marketing Research (Multimedia Marketing Consortium, London) how research problems with Coca-Cola's New Coke proved fatal.

[3]You can see Coca-Cola talking about the research later in the video browser in Marketing CD ROM Title 5: Marketing Research, Multimedia Marketing Consortium, London.

product
decisions

- Don't customers buy products?
- What is product quality and how do you measure it?
- Why don't great products win all the time?
- What's the difference between a product line and a product mix?
- What is a product portfolio and how do you balance it?
- Could you manage the NPD process?
- How do new products enter a market? What is the key?
- Do product life cycles really exist?
- How can a product designer create competitive advantage?
- How can a pack designer create competitive advantage?
- How does research help product design?
- How can pack research help to create competitive advantage?

Don't customers buy products?

Although 'product' in marketing terms can mean goods and services, we are going to concentrate on goods. In a pure marketing sense, products themselves have no value. But their benefits do. Customers buy benefits.

Although products are made in factories, what customers buy are benefits. Cars are bought not because they are cars, but because they deliver a number of benefits including transport, independence, status and image. Different market segments buy for different reasons. Just look at the range of different benefits offered in advertisements.

There is usually a core reason or benefit at the heart of every product purchase that ultimately satisfies an aroused need. This is intangible (you cannot touch it or feel it) and is referred to as the core product. Driving a particular car may make you feel good, powerful, successful or maybe it just takes you to work.

Beyond the intangible or non-physical core benefit, products have a tangible dimension. These are the physical aspects of the product: its features, quality level, design, packaging, and so on. This is the actual tangible product (the part of the product you can touch and feel).

On top of this tangible product are more intangibles which augment or increase the value of the product. Called the 'augmented product', this can include guarantees and services like credit facilities, delivery, installation, training, advice, servicing, insurance, and more.

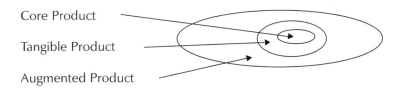

Core Product

Tangible Product

Augmented Product

Different markets need different amounts of intangibles to support the basic product. The trick is not to waste resources where they are not required or where they do not contribute to competitive advantage.[1]

In some markets, the tangible products are basically the same and the 'core' differences are only found in the intangibles. As markets change, the role played by the intangibles also changes. For a radically new product, for example, intangibles such as installation and training may be vital to successful customer adoption.

A more mature market, on the other hand, may require less intangibles. Alternatively, more intangibles might just create a competitive advantage.

In addition to the different layers of the product, there are also many different types of products, for example, organizational and consumer products. Take drills. There are domestic DIY drills and industrial drills. Industrial drills are a capital item. Some drills, like large heavy engineering drills, are often manufactured specifically to suit a particular customer's requirement. Going back to consumer products, these can be categorized by perishability or durability. Consumer durables like televisions and fridges are very different from non-durables like cans of beans and fresh fruit – called FMCGs, fast moving consumer goods.

There are many other product categories. They are all useful because each one has different buyer behaviour implications for the marketing mix. Whichever way they are categorized, remember that all three product elements – core, actual and augmented – with their tangible and intangible dimensions, have to be shaped and reshaped to meet the needs of the market. But in the customers' eyes they are all just part of the product.

> **"**In the factory we make cosmetics, in the market we sell hope.**"**
>
> *Charles Revlon*

What is product quality and how do you measure it?

What is quality? What does it mean to you? What does it mean to customers? Excellence? A degree of excellence? What degree of excellence? Do customers really care about the highest level of excellence, or do they just want a reasonable product that does the job reasonably well?

Or should quality exceed the customer's wildest dreams? Would it cost too much? Is it worth it? Does it deliver a significant competitive advantage? Would customers pay for it? Would they value it? Can competition copy it?

Should Lada cars try to build and deliver Rolls Royces? Do their customers expect a Rolls Royce? No, but they do expect a car that performs reasonably well. If they get that as a minimum, then they are satisfied and more likely to buy again. So quality is about customer expectations and perceptions as well as actual performance. Expectation of quality can be created and controlled by advertising and other marketing activities. Product quality should match the quality promised by all of the marketing mix.

Match it and you have satisfied customers who are more likely to buy again. Miss it and you have dissatisfied customers who are not only lost forever, but who also advise their friends not to buy. Exceed it and you have delighted customers. So always deliver at least the promised quality. And if you're not delivering it – you've either got to lower expectations or increase quality levels.

The producers of quality products tend to have an appreciation of the power of excellent design: aesthetics and functionality, performance and ergonomics, ease of assembly and disassembly, and more. This means the way a product looks, works and feels can all be improved by design. A well-designed product is not only cheaper to produce, but it also has a lot more value than a poorly designed product – provided it meets customer needs. Good design ensures that manufacturers design 'quality in' rather than just 'inspect faults out'.

There has to be consistency in the manufacture and delivery of that quality. This involves setting quality standards and motivating employees to meet them. Quality affects customer satisfaction, loyalty and retention, which in turn affect the company's financial performance. For example, moving from 94 per cent customer retention to 98 per cent retention can double profit levels. Quality, loyalty and retention figures are key indicators of future performance.

Managers may measure quality by counting product defects, customer complaints, satisfaction surveys and loyalty scores. Customers, however, perceive quality from more than just these factors. A quality image is conferred upon companies that not only produce great products, but also act as good corporate citizens who act in a socially responsible manner. A quality orientated organization instils quality into everything it does.

The quality issue is therefore a long-term strategic issue. It is not a short-term, ad hoc, occasional item on the agenda. A quality policy affects the long-term market position of the company.

Defining and measuring quality are worthwhile exercises

'Design quality in' (into the product) is better than 'inspect faults out'.

Why don't great products win all the time?

Over a hundred years ago Ralph Waldo Emerson suggested that 'If a man can write a better book, preach a better sermon, or make a better mousetrap than his neighbour, though he builds his house in the woods the world will make a beaten path to his door'.

This is certainly not true today. Many excellent products fail because no one knows about them, or they are wrongly positioned, or they're not available when people want them or they're too expensive for the chosen target market.

Other excellent products fail because a competitor's lower priced and inferior product is widely available before you even get to launch your product on the marketplace. Better mousetraps are often beaten by poorer mousetraps. It happens all the time.

Competitors constantly juggle their marketing mixes to maximize their product sales. Speed to market, blocked distribution channels, clever pricing strategies and powerful promotions are all used by competitors to win and keep market share.

The better mousetrap also needs to be part of a coherent, fully integrated marketing mix. The distribution has to get the product to where the target customer can buy it, when they want it. The prices have to reflect the desired quality image while simultaneously matching what customers can afford. Finally, customers need to know about the product – it needs to be promoted in the right way.

Each element of the marketing mix should support the product's positioning. The product, its price, its distribution channels and, of course, the promotion should all reinforce the same message. Without a coherent, fully integrated mix even the best product in the world will fail.

Going back to the Emerson's better mousetrap, ironically the best product is not always the best option. For example, the product might be so good that it costs too much to produce and therefore the best product might just put you out of business.

Ask yourself whether your customers really want that extra feature? Can you afford it? Can they afford it? Can the competition copy it? Whatever the decision, the final combination of the core product, tangible product and augmented product along with price, promotion and distribution need to work together if a product is to be successful.

Many excellent products fail, if the rest of the marketing mix isn't right

What's the difference between a product line and a product mix?

There are few single-product companies. Many companies start up as a single-product company, but they soon develop other products as the company grows and markets fragment. A product line is a string of products grouped together for marketing or technical reasons. Guinness started as a single-product company. Since then Guinness have extended the product line to fill market needs as they emerged. They have also expanded beyond the basic product line of beers. They also offer whiskeys, soft drinks and more... different lines of product.

Add all the product lines together and you get the product mix. Finding the right product mix is a subtle balancing act. How far should a product line be extended? How many different lines should be in the product group?

Line extension is attractive but dangerous. There are advantages and disadvantages lurking behind this apparently easy option. It is one of many different ways of increasing sales, extending an existing brand name onto a new product. Some feel that this reduces the risk of launching an unknown brand. Using a recognized brand name on a new product can give the new product immediate presence in the marketplace – customers can recognize, trust and try the new product more easily. This also creates savings in advertising and other promotions. So as the original product brand matures, the extended brand ensures some continuity and survival of the brand in the longer run.

Brand extension is a tempting option as it uses the same sales team with the same distribution channels and often the same customers. It can also fill or occupy any unoccupied positions in the market that might otherwise invite unwanted competitors into the market.

Finally, a full product line builds the image of the complete player, a big player, which in turn suggests reliability. But there are disadvantages lurking behind brand extensions and line extensions. A low-quality product will damage the original brand's reputation. A really good new product can also cannibalize the original product if the new product merely takes sales away from the old product. When contemplating brand extension, ask how much of the 'extra sales' actually replace existing sales of the original product? Constant brand extensions may dilute the brand's strength, its unique positioning, particularly if the extensions are not appropriate to the central brand. The marketer's task of being the guardian of the brand is a challenging one.

And so is the task of product extinction – phasing out and deleting products that have had their day. Having decided which products should be deleted, they have to be withdrawn carefully and gracefully without damaging employee morale or upsetting small groups of customers who may still want spare parts.

In a sense, product deletion should be a standard activity as companies constantly replace old products with improved ones.[2] The product portfolio section on the next page looks at this in more detail.

Extending the product line

Add all the product lines together and you get the product mix

What is a product portfolio and how do you balance it?

When a company grows it can find that it has many different products in many different markets. Senior managers need to be able to see the big picture of how they all fit together. Sometimes it can be difficult to see which products in which markets should be nurtured for growth and which ones deleted.

Igor Ansoff created four classic growth options: market penetration through increased market share – marketing existing products into existing markets; market development through marketing existing products into new markets; product development through creating and launching new products into existing markets; and diversification, the riskiest option of all, launching new products into new markets.[3]

The Ansoff matrix helps to categorize the options, but managers still need to know how these options affect cash and human resources as too little of either could starve a potential winning product of the resources it requires for successful growth.

This is where the Boston matrix can help to analyse the product portfolio. Senior managers need to know which products generate surplus cash, which ones need extra marketing budgets to support them and which ones should be deleted. They also need to know if they can fund new product development.

Products in growth markets generally require cash to support them to grow as cash gets tied up in working capital (stocks and debtors). Products which enjoy relatively large market shares in low-growth/mature markets are the 'cash cows' that generate the surplus cash that in turn funds other products, such as the high growth 'star' products. Although 'stars' enjoy large market shares in rapid growth markets, they need extra working capital funds if they are to keep pace with the overall market growth. They may, however, become tomorrow's cash cows when market growth eventually slows or matures and they have secured high market share. Products with a low share in a high growth market pose additional challenges and are called 'question marks'. Finally, low-growth, low-share products are called 'dogs' and sometimes absorb a disproportionate amount of management time.

Balancing the portfolio of products is crucial to long-term survival. New products are the lifeblood of the company's future. Old products eventually die. New products have to be introduced. This requires a delicate balancing act. Some companies, like Gillette, say that a minimum of 30 per cent of the company's sales should be generated through new products, that is products that are less than 5 years old.

Whether these are 'new products' or mere product improvements, modifications, brand extensions or genuine innovations depends on the company's attitude to risk, its ability to innovate and the resources available.

The section on product lines (on page 126) considers the problems of product development through brand extension. Meanwhile, remember that balancing the portfolio helps to secure the long-term future of the company.

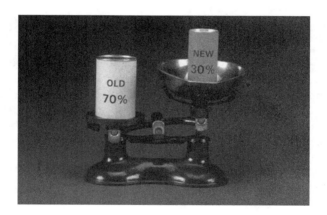

Some forward-looking companies insist that 30 per cent of all sales must come from new products

Could you manage the NPD process?

Most new products fail. The risk of failure can be reduced by establishing a sound NPD process or new product development process. Although there are variations, the basic process includes the following distinct stages.

Ideas are generated, screened, evaluated in more detail, developed, tested and finally launched.

Ideas come from everywhere. Whether from sophisticated social, anthropological or technical studies that reveal hidden needs and opportunities for new products or just ideas from brainstorming teams, suggestions from customers, distributors and employees.

Ideas are then screened to see how well they match the market's needs and simultaneously fit with the organization's overall objectives, strengths and resources.

The ideas that get through the initial screening are researched and developed into concepts for further evaluation. Although often presented on concept boards and researched in focus groups, some organizations, like Coca-Cola, carry out concept research among larger numbers of potential customers. The commercial viability of an idea is also evaluated by estimating costs, prices, sales, revenues, investment and profit.

The big spending then starts with the development stage. Teams of research and development specialists create prototype after prototype, testing and refining until they achieve the best solution.

To invest or not to invest. That is the question. A big investment goes into the tools that manufacture the final product. The tools can take six months to make. Once they are commissioned there is no turning back. This may require boardroom approval.

Meanwhile, marketing specialists develop the rest of the marketing mix. Brand names are registered, packaging designed, distribution channels selected, sales force briefed, and promotional activities prepared.

This is followed by testing – laboratory and real-life testing for safety and performance as well as market acceptance. If the results are positive, the product is launched usually on a 'roll-out' basis in one area after another, allowing demand and production to build up in a coordinated manner. The roll-out can also identify any last-minute hidden problems before going national or global.

The NPD process is not a linear sequence of events. Results from tests, customer feedback and general discussions send everyone back to the drawing board. So the NPD process is a series of loops rather than a linear process.

NPD plays a big continual part in a company's long-term success. Constant improvement of old products, along with the development of new ones, means companies like Sony produce 1000 new products per year or four new products each day. Their founder, Akio Morito, explained the underlying NPD drive when he said that his job was to make his products obsolete.

IDEA GENERATION

SCREENING

EVALUATION

DEVELOPMENT

TESTING

LAUNCH

(IMPROVEMENT)

The NPD process

"My job is to make my products obsolete."

Akio Morito, ex-Sony Chairman

How do new products enter a market? What is the key?

New products and new ideas are more appealing to some buyers than others. In fact, buyers can be segmented according to how much they like new ideas.

Research suggests that there is only a small percentage of buyers in consumer markets, about 2.5 per cent, that really like to be the first to try new products. They tend to be better educated and, in a sense, are always ready to risk buying an innovative product. Not surprisingly , they're called the 'innovators'.

There is another, much bigger group who also like to adopt innovative products, but only after seeing them being used and enjoyed by the innovators. This second and larger group of buyers is called the 'early adopters'. These opinion leaders represent about 13.5 per cent of all the eventual buyers and, because they tend to be very sociable, they influence other people.

After the first two groups have risked buying the new product the bulk of the market opens up. This is the majority of buyers. There are two groups within this majority: 'early majority' and the sceptics – the 'late majority'. Of equal size, their total represents about 68 per cent of all the buyers in a particular market.

There is one last group of buyers who appear to resist new products. In a sense they lag behind all the other buyers who by now have started buying the new product. These 'laggards' represent a significant number of buyers, about 16 per cent.

This is how innovations spread through a market – they move through a sequence of customer types from innovators to laggards. This is known as the diffusion of innovations. Here's another way of looking at it – imagine throwing a stone into a pond, watch what happens. After the splash, small waves ripple outwards from where the stone landed. Each wave creates another circle of wavelets, and so on. The diffusion of new products is a bit like this. There is a centre circle, a particular group of people who are the first to try a new product. They influence the next circle, or group of people, who, in turn, influence the next circle of people.

The key to the diffusion of innovations is to find the centre circles – the innovators and early adopters – and then spread out from there. Target the innovators and the early adopters first. Don't start with the laggards. These different circles of people have different profiles, media habits, lifestyles, levels of income, education and attitudes towards risk.

And as marketers get better at diffusing new products, services and ideas, product life cycles get shorter . There is an accelerated diffusion process as speed to market, reduced payback periods, shorter life cycles and ferocious competition combine to create a faster-moving model of diffusion. Electronically accelerated diffusion means using databases to profile and target each of the different types of buyer within the diffusion process.

Now if your new product has a global market, it may be worth considering whether some countries, or cultures, have more innovators than others. Could you target 'innovator cultures' in a global diffusion process?

Innovators and early adoptors actively seek out and enjoy new products

Do product life cycles really exist?

One of the most common concepts referred to in marketing is the product life cycle. Whether they are candles, horseshoes, hairnets or Harrier jets, products have life cycles. That means they all have a beginning… and an end.

Perhaps a little simplistic, but nevertheless it can provide a useful insight into a common pattern of total industry sales that the marketer must recognize. Businesses, like steam engine manufacturers, refused to see the end of their product's life cycle. They went out of business. They did not acknowledge the inevitable end of their product's life cycle.

Political, economic, social and technological changes affect product life cycles. The time frame can vary according to the industry, but the pattern remains the same: slow sales growth, rapid sales growth, mature sales and falling sales as the product is launched, grows rapidly, matures and eventually declines.

Although candles and horseshoes still exist today, their sales peaked long ago and are now minuscule compared to the vast volumes which were sold during previous centuries. Vinyl records and turntables had a shorter life cycle. Black-and-white TV had a relatively short cycle, which was extended by colour TV, but which is now near its decline stage as multimedia online PC/TVs emerge.

The marketing mix varies during each stage of the product life cycle. A product's life cycle can be extended by finding new users, new uses, increased usage and, of course, product modification.

New users mean new target markets. New uses for a product mean that new benefits and new ways of using the product have to be found. Increased usage is simply trying to get customers to increase their quantity and frequency of use.

Extended or not, the product life cycle is usually applied more easily to product form rather than product class or specific brands. For example, a product form such as black-and-white TV has a clearer life cycle than televisions in total, which is a product class.

Different products and whole industries have different time horizons, for example, the horseshoe's life cycle has had hundreds of years, while TV may have perhaps only 70.

The danger of over dependence on the life cycle means that a temporary dip in sales could trigger a premature withdrawal of a product – if the dip is misinterpreted as the final decline of the product.[4]

Finally, the life cycle is more descriptive than predictive. It describes the behaviour or sales pattern of a product as opposed to predicting its future sales precisely. Despite this limitation, the steam engine companies might just have survived in some manner or form if they'd been aware of where they were on the product life cycle and its fatal finality.

All products eventually die.

How can a product designer create competitive advantage?

Design affects everything – both form and function (the way things look and the way they work), what things cost and what they're worth. Almost all successful products come from good designs. Investment in design can create competitive advantage.

Designers can create radically new and exciting products. Design can also improve old ones by making them bigger and bolder, smaller and faster, safer and easier to use, store, service and recycle.

Design for disassembly means that some products are designed with a view to facilitating their ultimate recycling. Good design can even make products less expensive to produce and yet more reliable, 'increasing quality while reducing costs' – a nice challenge for a designer.

You name it and a good design team can probably do it. The skill is in the asking. Firstly, asking and convincing top management for the funds to invest in design, and secondly, asking or briefing the designer properly. Project management skills are needed to ensure that everyone keeps to schedule and operates within the budget.

Invested in, and managed carefully, good product design can create sustainable competitive advantage by creating both great products and cost-effective products. And remember, product design is not just about aesthetics, it's also about cost, reliability, materials conservation, ease of manufacture and ergonomics.

Product design is a powerful and often under-utilized resource just waiting to be tapped.

Product design – an underutilized resource

How can a pack designer create competitive advantage?

Customers see packaging as part of the product they buy. Good packaging design can create competitive advantage through lower costs, more attractive packs, more convenient packs, more protective packs and more environmentally friendly packs.

Ideally packs should communicate, protect and offer convenience to the user, buyer, transporter and distributor. The designer achieves all of these by blending the following five variables.

- Size
- Shape
- Colour
- Graphics
- Materials

Each of these variables affects each of the three basic functions of packaging: communication, protection and convenience. The pack acts as a silent sales representative, helping customers by bringing a certain benefit to their attention, highlighting USPs and giving friendly tips on usage.

Pack design is often evolutionary rather than revolutionary. This means the pack needs to be reviewed regularly as markets change. Design tweaks may appear unnoticeable, but are essential in order to keep the product abreast of the market. Good packaging design can deliver competitive advantage.

Some pack designs need to be evolutionary rather than revolutionary – design tweaks which keep the products abreast with the market

How does research help product design?

Good designers invest in research. Initial research into the marketplace, existing products, users and environments is followed by more focused research as they move into and refine subsequent product concepts. Some designers will spend weeks researching a particular product area. This may involve collecting pictures, ads and leaflets of other products. It may even involve collecting images of the environment in which the product may be used. And then they try to make sense of all the information and arrange the images into groups and clusters. Trends, patterns and gaps may emerge offering the designer new opportunities. There is much research to be carried out before attempting any actual design work. Here is Kevin Thompson of Grey Matter talking about their 'design wheel', which they use as an initial research tool before carrying out any design work whatsoever. In this case they are researching pots and pans for the kitchen.

> 'As a brand and product developers, we at Grey Matter work at the sharp end of new product development. The product wheel is a concept developed by Grey Matter, to help us and our clients to have a clearer understanding of the marketplace in which their products operate. The main purpose is to identify and clearly explain the visual cues and codes that operate in their particular market sectors.
>
> 'We also highlight future trends by identifying the key influences that affect the market, and examine their inter-relationships in any one particular market. The aim of this presentation technique is to place products in rank order against each other within a 3D flat space. I am going to demonstrate this using two visual wheels prepared for the Prestige Group based on the domestic UK market. The first wheel maps the environment in which the products are used. The wheel shows the various styles of kitchen common to the UK domestic market.'

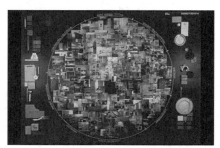

Design wheel mapping kitchen environments

'The centre of our wheel shows the mass market moving outwards to aspirational. So, at 12 o'clock round to 4 o'clock we have traditional wooden finishes flowing into new and emerging kitchen designs at 6 o'clock. This sector accounts for approximately 85 per cent of the UK market. From 6 o'clock we move into the minimalist kitchens evolving into psuedo professional at 8 o'clock, ending up with continental colours between 11 and 12 o'clock. Outside the perimeter of the wheel, we show 3D product samples that reflect the look and feel of the individual sectors. Now… if we focus on the continental colours, we see primary colours in the scrap art imagery supported by 3D samples showing stainless steel and highly decorated finishes.

'The next wheel maps stainless steel cookware. As before, the centre shows the mass market moving towards aspirational at the perimeter. We use the same descriptors as before so we can map the products against the environment wheel. If we could superimpose the two wheels they would correlate. The interesting feature of this wheel is the gaps in the product offers.'

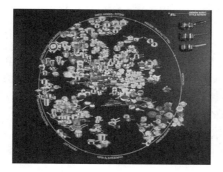

Design wheel mapping stainless steel cookware

'These could present opportunities for new product development. We find this type of visual mapping is much easier to understand and more useful than the traditional bi-polar mapping techniques.'

So there you have it. Careful research helps to identify better design solutions to market challenges.

How can pack research help to create competitive advantage?

Good designers should invest heavily in research. After establishing what is needed and being given a brief covering positioning, target markets, marketing mix, cost constraints, shelf constraints, deadlines and, of course, a budget, pack designers carry out different types of research.

Initial research into the environment is carried out – how the pack will be stored, stacked, poured and presented in both the store and the home. In-store research investigates the retail outlets in which the product is already distributed at present and also any outlets you intend moving into in the future.

A key research issue is lighting, because some stores are sometimes badly lit while others are very well lit. So the pack may have to fight in good lighting and bad lighting environments. The consumer has to recognize the pack on the shelf among the competition and among all the other products that are up against it on the shelf. The retailers' shelf space has to be researched – how much space will the product be allocated on the shelf?

Armed with the retail research, the designers can start to develop some ideas – in both two dimensions and three dimensions. Both 2D and 3D ideas, or 'concepts', are researched carefully before committing the organization to investing in the final packaging design.

Let's look at some of the five different concepts which design consultants, PI Design, created for Fisons Lawn Care Products:

- Concept 1, for instance, is aimed at the scientific consumer.
- Concept 2 is targeted at the consumer who has a vision of a rather pretty house and set of gardens.
- Concept 3 is even more romantic with an impressionist style.
- Concept 4 is aimed at somebody who looks at the garden as something to work in, something to nourish and something to relax in.
- Concept 5 is based upon a graphic whereby the consumer would aspire towards inviting some friends around and here we have an execution where the garden is somewhere to relax.

So we're trying to make a link between different people's perceptions of their gardens and the product achieving that event for them. Research eventually identified the pack (Concept 5) that was really communicating with the consumer the best and proved to be the most appealing concept.

It was around this concept, and the point that was making it successful was basically the large spread of lawn that really relates to the product that we're trying to promote... the goodness of your lawn.

This was then developed through to the final label, which had got the enormous spread of lawn with the house signalling English country homes in the background.

Simultaneous research is carried out into the three-dimensional concepts covering the pack's shape, size, materials and functions such as protection, convenience and communication. All of this research costs time and money, but it does increase the likelihood of success.

Notes

[1]Watch out for Peter Doyle in the video browser in Marketing CD ROM Title 6: Product Decisions (Multimedia Marketing Consortium, London) talking about product preference and the augmented product.

[2]See Kenichi Ohmae in the video browser in Marketing CD ROM Title 6: Product Decisions (Multimedia Marketing Consortium, London) talking about Obsoleting Strategies! The section on the Product Portfolio considers how to balance product lines and mixes, old and new.

[3]Watch out for Kenichi Ohmae in the video browser in Marketing CD ROM Title 6: Product Decisions (Multimedia Marketing Consortium, London) when he talks about how he reduces the axes of risk.

[4]Peter Doyle, explains his dislike for the concept in the video browser in Marketing CD ROM Title 6: Product Decisions, Multimedia Marketing Consortium, London.

service
decisions

- Why are service industries growing so fast?
- What are the five characteristics that separate products from services?
- What category of service are you in?
- How do you measure quality in services?
- Why are the 4Ps inadequate when marketing services?
- How does looking after employees pay dividends?
- How does physical evidence psychologically influence buyers?
- How can low-contact activities be separated from high-contact activities?
- Should you extend your range of services or not?
- How do you distribute a service?
- How are services promoted?
- Why is pricing a service different to pricing a product?

Why are service industries growing so fast?

Services offer more job opportunities and more growth potential than the marketing of goods. In Japan, the USA and Europe more people already work in services than manufacturing. And the figure is growing.

Sales of services in both consumer and organizational markets are expanding. At home and overseas services are also being exported – in fact they are the fastest growing part of international trade.

Why? Freedom.

Freeing up personal time and freeing up business overheads. Consumers want services that free up their leisure time, and organizations want services that free up their overhead costs.

Take organizations. Subcontracting, out-sourcing, down-sizing or right-sizing – call it what you want – organizations today buy in more services from outside than ever before. Instead of having their own staff and equipment, they buy in many of those services as required.

Fixed overheads are cut by releasing staff and equipment tied up in canteens, computers, warehouses and delivery vehicles. Buying in services changes costs from fixed overheads to flexible variable costs.

As the organization slims down, it becomes what Charles Handy calls 'a box of contracts' with most activities contracted out. By shedding the activities that they are not especially good at, organizations can focus on what they are excellent at – their core competencies.

The other activities, at which they are less competent, can be carried out by an outside supplier in a much more efficient and cost effective way. This has led to 'network organizations', where access to skills is more important than ownership of those skills.

Now consider consumer markets – they also want more services. Longer working weeks and dual-income families mean less leisure time. Services like baby-minding free up work time, while services like cleaning and ironing free up limited leisure time. In a sense, consumers buy time when buying services. Time will continue to grow in importance. Customers are increasingly interested in saving time. And with greater affluence, consumers can now also afford to buy other services, some of which were once considered only available to the rich.

Services in both domestic and organizational markets are growing and so too are the demands on the marketing managers that supply them. The marketing of a service involves the management of people, productivity, the process of producing the service, quality and physical evidence as well as the other typical marketing activities.

There are separate sections on each of these areas, which are essential in the quest for success in the marketing of services.

In the marketing of both services and products, service elements are key differentiators.

What are the five characteristics that separate products from services?

Services are not the same as goods, although many goods have services attached to them and vice versa. The major characteristics of services are: intangibility, inseparability, perishability, variability and ownership.

Take intangibility. Services are intangible. You cannot pick them up and inspect their quality before purchase. They are low in 'search qualities' – tangible clues that can be evaluated before purchase. In fact, customers have few objective measures for evaluating many services. In a sense, many buyers just buy confidence in a service.

Customers without prior experience depend on the company's image, its literature, physical evidence and other people's opinions – the power of word of mouth.

Buyers with experience draw upon experience qualities – previous experiences of the service in terms of say, speed, friendliness, performance, and so on. But even with experience, performance may still be difficult to measure. How do you know if your car service, face lift or rewiring is of high quality?

These are 'credence qualities' – features that are hard to evaluate even after the event. These often abstract variables make buying services more risky. This is why customers look for visual cues – physical evidence of quality. Is the area clean, orderly and comforting or dirty, confusing and upsetting? The service environment is never neutral.

In addition to intangibility, another characteristic of services is inseparability of production and consumption as they usually occur simultaneously. This makes the delivery of consistent quality standards more challenging as uncontrollable variables, such as customers, are involved in both production and consumption.

As customers and producers have a lot of contact, staff training and motivation become vital as quality staff can create differential advantage over competitors. People perform differently depending on the time of day, week, month or year. This makes every service delivered at least a little bit different.

This variability, or heterogeneity, makes it difficult to standardize the quality of services. And no matter how good the service is, you can't save it or store it. Services are extremely perishable. An unsold seat on an airline is revenue lost forever. There are no stocks only unsold seats.

Even when bought, services are never owned by the customer. Buyers only buy temporary access to the service.

So services are highly perishable, heterogeneous, intangible performances simultaneously produced and consumed, that cannot be stored and are never owned. You'd wonder why people buy them!

This makes the delivery of consistent quality standards more challenging since uncontrollable variables, such as customers, are involved in both production and consumption

What category of service are you in?

There are many different types of services. Some are labour intensive, skill intensive or equipment intensive. And some are a mixture of both man and machine. Some are place bound, while others are time bound.

Many service suppliers search for ways to replace repetitive labour activities with automated facilities. But some skilled services cannot be replaced by machines – yet. And the level of skill required can vary across different types of services; for example, drilling a road obviously requires different skills from drilling a tooth.

Other skill intensive services like beauty therapy, or management consultancy, require little or no equipment. On the other hand, there are skill-intensive services, like cosmetic surgery, that use a blend of both skill and equipment with high-tech lasers being used by skilled consultants.

The time taken to complete these services can vary. Other services, like horse riding or helicopter training, are time bound in that the service requires a certain minimum amount of contact time between customer and supplier.

Incidentally, the section on processes (on page 157) explains how and why some services try to separate 'contact activities', like customer service, from the other 'behind the scene' activities, like administration.

Some services can only be supplied in certain places. These are place bound and include services such as adventure holidays. The section on service distribution looks at the constraints of place and whether this barrier to growth can be reversed by mobilizing and decentralizing the service.

The level of customization versus standardization is another criteria that can be used to categorize services. So there are many approaches to categorize services including levels of labour, equipment, skill, contact time, place and customization. Categorizing services helps to identify the common issues and gain strategic insights into the marketing of services.

> **"**Some skilled services cannot be replaced by machines – YET. 'In the 21st century there won't be a clear difference between human beings and robots.'**"**
>
> *Ray Kurzweil*[1]

How do you measure quality in services?

Managing levels of quality in services is more difficult than for goods for at least two reasons: intangibility and individuality. Whereas goods have tangible quality standards like size and weight, services have more abstract quality standards like time and happiness, for example, queuing times and satisfaction scores respectively.

In addition, the individuality of employees and customers means quality, both real and perceived, can vary. The inseparability of production and consumption of services means customers can participate in the process of delivery.

This means the quality of the service is partly dependent on customer performance. Customer adherence to rules and regulations can affect the quality image, eg customers who insist on smoking, shouting or misbehaving in a restaurant. Equally, the perceived quality of a self-service restaurant is very low if it is untidy – regardless of who makes the mess, whether it's customers or staff.

The individuality of employees' and customers' performances complicates the quality equation and deepens the marketer's fascination with human nature and its effect on service quality.

So how do you define and measure quality in services? There are many criteria but here are five: reliability, responsiveness, assurance, empathy and tangibles.

Tangibles include physical evidence such as staff, uniforms, buildings – do they project the desired quality image? High scores across all these criteria would be very nice. It may even differentiate your service from the competition, but can you afford it and does the customer want it? Will they pay for it? And does the level of service match the desired positioning?

Quality control has a major impact on the financial situation. Research shows that on average businesses with poor service quality ratings earn low margins and lose market share each year. On the other hand, high-quality businesses gain market share and enjoy higher margins.

Quality is all about expectations and subsequent performance. Customer expectations are created, firstly, by the promises made in advertisements and other communication tools, and secondly, by customers' previous experiences.

Performance is primarily delivered by staff. You can see how they influence quality in the section on people. Services are high in credence qualities – which makes measuring quality, even after the event, difficult.

Customer expectations and subsequent perceptions about quality are often based on their unquantifiable subjective feelings. Marketing managers, on the other hand, can objectively measure (through surveys) and maintain high levels of quality in services if there is a quality orientation, a customer orientation and an overall marketing orientation permeating every aspect of the organization.

Quality of service can and should be measured

Why are the 4Ps inadequate when marketing services?

One of the most common approaches to the marketing mix for products is Jerome McCarthy's 4Ps. Product, price, place and promotion are combined together in such a way that customers can learn about a product and buy it at an affordable price from a convenient place.

But the 4Ps are not enough for services. Because of their intangibility, perishability, variability and inseparability combined with simultaneous production and consumption, services also need to expand the mix to accommodate other key ingredients required by successful services. Booms and Bitner[2] added 3Ps: physical evidence, people and processes of producing the service.

Firstly, the physical evidence includes the way a place of service looks, feels and smells. These can influence a customer even before entering the place of service.

Secondly, the people, or staff, who produce the service are really front-line marketing people as well as production people. The staff behind the counter are the organization's ambassadors – part of its PR team. They are also part of the marketing research team, sales team and marketing team. Staff have many responsibilities and much potential.

Thirdly, the process of actually producing the service. Customers can see it all, or at least a lot of the process. They can also participate in the process, depending on how much a manager wants to save money and involve them as part of the experience they buy. Whatever the process, it should make it easy to do business – in other words the process should help and not hinder.

To conclude, there are many similarities in the marketing of goods and services. Aspects of all three of the services 'extra' Ps may be present in the marketing of goods. It is, however, the different emphasis of physical evidence, people and the process of production that make the marketing of services a little different from the marketing of goods.

Physical evidence, process (of producing the service) and people that deliver it add extra dimensions

How does looking after employees pay dividends?

People play a vital role in the marketing of services. In fact, they are both producers and marketers of the service as they have direct contact with customers. They are the ambassadors of the organization.

Although the level of contact varies according to the type of service – whether it is time intensive, skill intensive, machine intensive – the customer almost always comes into contact with people who produce all, or at least some, of the service.

These front-line staff influence a customer's experiences and perceptions about the service. They can make a customer feel good or bad, partly by the actual quality of the service and partly by their attitude, interest and enthusiasm. Employee enthusiasm is a reflection of how they are treated, trained and rewarded.

Happy employees create happy customers who want to come back again and again. Heskett's service quality wheel[3] develops this: employees who feel involved and rewarded deliver more customer satisfaction, which creates increased volume of business, which both satisfies and further motivates employees, and on it goes.

Bill Marriot, of Marriot Hotels, once asked, 'How can we have happy customers without happy employees?'

Looking after employees pays dividends. Literally. An 11-year research project, by Harvard professors Kotter and Heskett, revealed that companies who value their employees as much as their customers and their shareholders vastly outperform those that don't by over six times in sales and nine times in share price.

Although some of the people involved in delivering services are behind the scenes (in administration), a true marketing/customer service orientation reaches over the shoulders of the front-line servers and into the back rooms where organizational structures, operational systems and management structures reside. These people also help to deliver quality.

Recruitment, training, motivation and communication are the building blocks for success. Human resource management skills are vital in services. Internal marketing needs to be vigilant in constantly reminding staff of the importance of good service. And remember, external marketing, like advertising, can also influence internal staff.

Carefully recruited, properly trained and reasonably rewarded staff become motivated and make a difference. They can help to differentiate an organization's service from the many others out there. This can create competitive advantage, or differential advantage. Elaborate customer care costs money. Do customers really want it? Can the company afford it? However, it is worth remembering that some aspects of customer service, like smiling, cost nothing.

Happy Employees = Happy Customers = Happy Shareholders.

How does physical evidence psychologically influence buyers?

To buy or not to buy, that is the question.

Some services get a resolute 'no' just because of the way the building or staff appear. When buying intangible services, customers often need tangible or physical evidence as an indicator of service quality.

The physical environment in which a service is presented and executed influences buyers. Even before they set foot inside. The decision to enter or not to enter is made outside. This decision is often made solely on the store's visual image. The final decision to buy is often made inside the store. Clues about retail outlets are absorbed, often without knowing it. Psychologists call these 'cue patterns'. These help buyers to decide what kind of shop it is without actually entering.

Once inside, the buyer looks for other cues or clues about the quality of service. Levels of cleanliness, spaciousness, comfort, combined with colours, graphics, music, aromas, design and layout send messages to the buyer. Here, marketers are interested in the physical environment, because here appeals can be made to all the senses. Marketing messages are not confined to the limited dimensions of many other advertising media.

On the other hand, there are a lot more variables to be managed here. That means attention to detail.

Customers take messages where sometimes none are intended. A dirty ashtray, a missing button, an untidy desk, a cobweb or a spider and even other customers all convey messages about the quality of the service.

And, of course, staff have a major role in the physical environment. Their uniforms, the way they look, the way they walk, talk and act in general. The section on people considers this in more detail.

Interior and exterior design also plays an important part in the marketing of services. Buildings are permanent media that make suggestions about the organization and its services. Do the buildings reinforce the positioning strategy? Are they seen to be futuristic, hi-tech, traditional, big or small, fast or caring? Does the building convey an image that matches the desired corporate image?

Since services are basically low in tangible 'search characteristics' (characteristics that help buyers to evaluate products before buying), customers still look for any tangible clues to help to judge the quality of a service.

The physical environment provides a host of clues that help to reduce the additional risk that buyers suffer when buying services. The physical environment can also enhance the experience qualities and the credence qualities upon which the marketing of services are so dependent.

So, the physical environment, along with people and process form the additional 3Ps which are essential elements in the marketing mix for services.

Interior and exterior design send messages to customers

How can low-contact activities be separated from high-contact activities?

Some products would lose their romance and mystery, whereas others would never be bought, if customers ever saw the reality of the production process. A product's manufacturing process is usually hidden behind closed doors away from the prying eyes of customers.

Services and their production processes, on the other hand, are exposed to the public at large because production and consumption are basically simultaneous. Customers see the 'production process' or at least some of it, since their consumption is part of production. Without their participation the service could not be produced.

The nature and level of customer participation is determined by the type of service, the level of skill, time and contact required. Dry cleaning and acupuncture provide a useful contrast.

Most services have a mixture of high- and low-contact activities. The bulk of the dry cleaning services are done without the customer being present (maybe in a back room), while the acupuncture service is performed in the presence of the customer. The invoicing and appointment making may be done again in the back room without the customer's presence.

The trick, as Peter Doyle[4] suggests, is to separate the two activities and then 'maximize the efficiency of the low-contact activity and maximize the effectiveness of the high-contact activity'.

That means increasing productivity in low-contact activities through, say, automation and increasing quality of high-contact activities with warmer greetings, nicer environments, and so on. Some of the low-contact activities can be processed in batch production to gain economies.

There are other production-line approaches being used in services. Machinery, robotics and computers combine to automate services such as car washes and cash dispensers.

Other efficiencies can be gained from developing low-tech systems such as self-service or fast-food production systems. It is here that customer participation can gain further efficiencies. Customers are often prepared to queue for food, carry it themselves, eat without cutlery and afterwards clear their own table – all without a tip!

One of the key skills in managing the service process is managing the peaks and troughs of demand against the relatively fixed supply. Off-peak offers can help with the demand. The supply side of the equation may prove more challenging.

Flexi hours, part-time staff, more motivated and competent staff capable of sustaining a 'two-hour rush', and some shared services or strategic alliances can ease supply problems. People play a big part in the overall process of delivering services. Understanding and managing people is a key skill.

The section on 'How does looking after employees pay dividends? (page 153) looks at their important role in the marketing of services.

"Maximize the efficiency of the low contact activity and maximize the effectiveness of the high contact activity.**"**

Professor Peter Doyle[5]

Should you extend your range of services or not?

Just like product markets, there are few-single service organizations that focus on one service only. Growth can come from adding on new products or services by extending the line or mix of services on offer.

Take Manchester United Football Club. They provide an entertainment service. But like many football clubs they realize the potential for boosting sales and profits by adding new lines to their core service.

Here is their club secretary, Ken Merrett.

> 'Well, we obviously market football as our main core, but there's all the offshoots, such as merchandising, the sale of space in the executives' accommodation. We have lounges which accommodate up to 500 people, we have a museum and tours department, membership, anything which is connected remotely with football we market.'[6]

Should the service organization become a multi-service organization? Does the organization's reputation and skills and other resources lend themselves to develop other services? Does it create synergy? Or does it take them into uncharted territory? Does it dilute their brand or enhance it? Does it match existing customers' requirements or does it take the organization into new target markets... more uncharted territory that increases the axis of risk?[7]

So which services should be added? Decisions about the service mix are difficult ones and require a senior management perspective. Various matrices like Ansoff's growth matrix, or the Boston Consulting Group's matrix help to analyse the routes for growth and the optimum balance of new services to old services.

Getting the right balance or portfolio of services is a long-term strategic issue. It involves strategic decisions about target markets, positioning and capital investment.

Extending the line and mix of services has advantages and disadvantages. Using a recognized brand name helps customers to trust and try a new service, while simultaneously it saves the organization money on advertising and promotions. But brand extensions also have some inherent disadvantages.

A new service with low quality can damage the reputation of the other services. And even good-quality services can damage sales by cannibalizing or taking sales away from the old service.

However, extending the line is seen by some as a strategic competitive weapon in that the new services fill in any gaps that might otherwise invite unwanted competition into the marketplace. A large portfolio of services also gives the impression of being a major and reliable service supplier.

So service-mix decisions have long-term strategic impact and require careful consideration.

> **"**You should never take many axes of risk simultaneously. To sell something unknown to unknown territories through unknown channels.**"**
>
> *Kenichi Ohmae*[8]

How do you distribute a service?

Sooner or later successful services face some difficult distribution questions such as: 'What is the best distribution strategy? Are there any distribution barriers?'

Many services sell and perform their services directly to customers at the place where the service is provided. Growth can be constrained by the ability to sell to and service their customers from a single site. Several distribution options emerge. For example: indirect distribution; direct distribution; and breaking 'place bound' barriers.

Distribution can be increased indirectly through agents like travel and ticket agents. Direct distribution can be increased directly by increasing the number of sites either through wholly owned sites or by franchised sites.

A single site can also increase its capacity to distribute its services by increasing 'back office' activities such as direct mail and telephone selling. But growth is still limited by the capacity to perform the service on the site.

This begs a big question. Is the service 'site bound'? Do customers have to come to the service or can the service come to customers? Doctors, nurses, teachers, mechanics, therapists, even restaurants already reverse their distribution by bringing the service to the customer or providing in-home services.

Developments in information technology will lead to new distribution channels in many services like banking, counselling and consultancy as ATMs, phones, TVs, PCs, multimedia kiosks and the Internet interact and integrate.

A radical shift in the distribution of services can affect costs, but can also create a sustainable competitive advantage while expanding the distribution network. Obviously, if the service is equipment-based the question of mobility is more challenging but not insurmountable.

The next question becomes financial. Does home delivery / office delivery cost more? Probably more in variable costs of travel, but less in reduced fixed overheads as the service requires less premises. Do customers want the home service? For example, eating out and eating in are two different experiences.

As the service expands through whatever distribution option, control becomes a more interesting management challenge. How do you control quality levels? Should sales and servicing be rigorously and centrally controlled, or should it be decentralized and spread out so that everyone is responsible for adhering to the organization's quality standards and procedures?

To centralize or not to centralize? To be place bound or not? To go direct or indirect? To franchise or not to franchise? These are just some of the distribution dilemmas involved in services.

Many services break the traditional 'site bound' barriers

Growth can be constrained by the ability to seek and service customers from a single site

How are services promoted?

Nothing communicates quite like the product itself, or in this case, the service itself. A high-quality service creates a strong platform for promotion. This is particularly true with services as they are high in experience and credence qualities.

This means that previous experiences of the service are recalled when deciding to buy again. Other people's experiences are also called upon – such as a friend's opinion. The actual quality of the service creates the 'experience values'. This is why all staff are really part of the sales team.

'Credence values' are those values that are hard to evaluate even after the service. Post-sales service, correspondence, direct mail and telemarketing all help to cement the relationship if used correctly.

Customers are also sometimes influenced by certificates and awards on the wall, levels of authority and confidence demonstrated during the service, the atmosphere and the overall corporate image behind the service. All of these can arouse feelings of security and suggestions of quality.

Word of mouth is a powerful persuader. Customers talk to each other. Dissatisfied customers tell at least two or three times more people than do satisfied customers. You can see why service companies try to get their customers to tell them first about any problems or complaints. Some customers are obviously more talkative than others. Some are opinion leaders, or opinion formers, who actively spread messages to their opinion followers. So identifying and communicating with opinion leaders makes sense. Marketers are aware of the potent power of word of mouth. They have many tools such as 'friend get friend' or 'neighbour get neighbour' campaigns, where customers are rewarded for introducing a friend as a new customer. T-shirts, postcards, in-store photographs, bulletin boards on the Internet, publicity stunts and creative advertising stimulate word of mouth discussions among customers. Everything communicates: the service, the store, the uniform, the staff, the building – even the bill.

The next question is what to communicate? What message? This depends on the positioning strategy – how you want the service to be seen? It also depends on the target market. What do they need to know? What benefits are they forgetting about or don't know about yet?[9]

But remember, don't promise what you can't deliver. Don't disappoint customers in your attempt to attract them. Meet and exceed expectations and you will develop long-lasting relationships.

There is always room for creativity

Finally, consider Lynn Shostack's 'opposites'[10] – an intangible service should be promoted with tangibles and a tangible good promoted with intangible ideas. This means that communications can include tangibles like buildings, people, logos and any tangible goods that are part of the overall service.

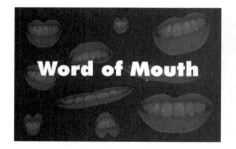 

Word of mouth is a powerful persuader

Why is pricing a service different to pricing a product?

Price is a multifaceted tool in the marketing of services. It communicates quality levels, it controls demand and, of course, it can be used as a loss leader to promote or cross-sell other services.

Price can be used as an indicator of quality. Many insecure buyers will read a high price tag as a quality tag. In the absence of other objective information price has a psychological value.

Customers buying services are renowned for their lack of objective evaluation because service is intangible and intangibles are difficult to measure with hard criteria. So price often communicates messages about quality.

Price also helps to solve the bottlenecks of limited facilities. Given the fixed capacity of most services, pricing can be used to help to cope with fluctuating demand. Excess demand during peak time can be channelled into a less busy period by offering special rates. Low prices can also be used to stimulate demand during off-peak periods.

Prices are often bundled and spread across a range of services. They can be used as loss leaders to entice customers into buying a service at a very low price with a view to eventually buying other services (cross-selling).

Understanding segmentation is crucial to using pricing effectively as a tool in service marketing. Different segments pay different prices. One problem with setting prices for services is calculating costs.

These can be complicated because of the simultaneous production/consumption nature of services. It can be difficult to calculate exactly how long a customer will take to consume the service, hence the difficulty of assessing the total cost.

Some services like consultants within professional fields charge an hourly rate, while others such as dental practices have more guidance with fixed fees for different treatments.

Finally, the perishability of services means there is a constant temptation towards contribution pricing. An empty seat is revenue lost for ever, so any revenue raised, no matter how small, makes some contribution towards the overall fixed costs of the company. But the 'something is better than nothing' principle can sink a service if applied continuously, because overheads may never be fully covered.

So the pricing of services is distinct from product pricing in its many hidden complications and challenges for the marketing manager.

Price is a multifaceted tool in the marketing of services

Notes

[1]Kurzweil, R (1999) in *The Age Of Spiritual Machines*, Viking Press.

[2]Booms, B H and Bitner, M J (1981) in Marketing strategies and organizational structures for service firms in *Marketing of Services*, ed J Donnelly and W R George, pp 47–51, American Marketing Association, Chicago.

[3]Kotter, P and Heskett, J (1992) *Corporate Culture and Performance*, Free Press, New York.

[4]Doyle, P (1996) Marketing CD ROM Title 7: Service Decisions, Multimedia Marketing Consortium, London.

[5]Doyle, P (1999) Marketing CD ROM Title 7: Service Decisions, Multimedia Marketing Consortium, London.

[6]Merrett, K (1999) Marketing CD ROM Title 7: Service Decisions, Multimedia Marketing Consortium, London.

[7]You can see Ohmae on the axes of risk later in the video browser in Marketing CD ROM Title 7: Service Decisions, Multimedia Marketing Consortium, London.

[8]Ohmae, K (1999) Marketing CD ROM Title 7: Service Decisions, Multimedia Marketing Consortium, London.

[9]You can see how SouthWestern Bell research this later in the video browser in Marketing CD ROM Title 7: Service Decisions, Multimedia Marketing Consortium, London.

[10]Shostack, G L (1977) Breaking free from product marketing, *Journal of Marketing*, April, pp 73–80.

pricing
decisions

- Is price simply what the customer will pay, or is it a more flexible marketing tool?
- What is your pricing objective?
- What is your pricing strategy?
- If a product retails at £9.99, what price can a manufacturer charge?
- What are Ohmae's 3Cs which influence pricing?
- How many different types of costs are there?
- Why should you avoid a price war at all costs?
- Don't all customers feel the same about prices?
- Why is a cost-orientated approach to pricing wrong?
- What is the market-orientated approach to pricing?
- What is the systematic approach to pricing?
- What are the kinds of problems that relate to pricing?

Is price simply what the customer will pay, or is it a more flexible marketing tool?

Tomorrow morning you are going to wake up, have breakfast and leave the house. On the way to the bus stop or the station you will buy a newspaper. Which one? The prices are different. How much will you pay?

Prices vary according to situations. Different prices reflect what different customers are prepared and able to pay. But is price simply what the customer will pay, or is it a more flexible marketing tool? Setting the right price can mean the difference between profit and loss, survival and failure.

The basic rule in pricing is to price your product or service at the level that your customers expect to pay for the quality you are delivering. This does not mean that high price means high quality. Nor does it mean that high quality will justify a high price.

Customers generally buy at a certain level of price and quality that is dictated by the social and psychological forces around them. Different segments are attracted by different price / quality levels. This is called the price–quality relationship. Ford and Rolls-Royce sell into different markets, but for most of their markets they are neither cheap nor expensive – they simply deliver the quality their customers expect at the price they expect to pay for it.

*Different segments are attracted by
different price/quality thresholds*

Pricing directly affects sales revenue. A company has to relate sales revenue to costs – cost of sales, cost of production, cost of raw materials and other costs, such as transport and promotion. So most companies try to run a long-term strategy for their pricing. World prices of raw materials can go up and down, but customers may expect the price to remain stable. Combining the product and the price is often referred to as the product–price mix. For example, consumers may be willing to pay more because there is good after-sales service. A brand that is well-supported by advertising will normally be able to command a higher price. Even when consumers have less money to spend, as in a recession, a strong well-supported brand is often able to command a premium price.

Price is also unique within the marketing mix in that it is the only ingredient in the mix that makes money. All the other ingredients incur cost. Yet many companies conduct little or no research into pricing. Most customers in any particular target market have similar perceptions of the price–quality relationship and this should be a main factor in developing prices.

Too high a price and sales might be too low. Too low a price and sales might be high but without profit. Effective marketing should include research into customers' attitudes towards not just the product, but also how they will value it. Value is a combination of price and perceived quality.

Understanding the price–quality relationship is vital in marketing.

Price and quality should match each other and not contradict each other

What is your pricing objective?

The pricing objectives set by companies are generally seeking to maximize sales revenue over costs and achieve profit. But market situations can vary. Philip Kotler[1] suggests that a company can pursue the following six major pricing objectives.

- Survival – is a typical objective of a company faced with intensive competition and not enough customers. Prices are set to cover variable costs and some fixed costs to ensure that the company stays in business.

- Maximum current profit – is where companies with weak competition set a high price that produces the most cash flow or return on investment.

- Maximum current revenue – is where companies set prices to maximize sales revenues – unit sales multiplied by unit price. Demand is calculated at different price points.

- Maximum sales growth – is where companies set low prices to achieve high unit sales so as to get lower unit cost and higher long-term profit. This is also called market penetration pricing.

- Market skimming – is where a company sets a high price to capture those customers who are willing to pay more for a product. It is skimming the cream off the top of the market, and it works well with an innovative or new technology product.

- Product quality leadership – is where a company aims to provide the best quality product in the market, and therefore charges more than its competitors. These companies are usually market leaders.

Pricing objectives for particular products or services can also vary according to the stage in the product life cycle. For example, in the decline stage a company may choose a harvesting strategy that gradually reduces expenditures on advertising and maybe even product quality, while maximizing profits by maintaining prices. Alternatively, in the decline stage the company might adopt a divesting strategy which looks for another organization to buy that part of the business.

Pricing objectives are never simple. They result from the company trying to balance a number of different business aims both short and long term –

such as market share, sales, profit and technical or quality leadership. These have to be considered so that the company is able both to survive and to achieve sound long-term profits.

Pricing objectives must fit in with the overall marketing objectives. They must fully integrate with and support all the other elements of the marketing mix. The next section on pricing strategies explains how objectives can be developed into meaningful strategies for the marketplace.

Pricing objectives may vary according to the stage in the product life cycle

What is your pricing strategy?

Whatever pricing objectives are adopted, there are various pricing strategies that can be used to achieve those objectives. Pricing strategies involve not only method and level of price, but also how this works with the rest of the marketing mix. Pricing strategies also depend on what is happening in the market and how the company wants to react to it. They can be defensive or aggressive, and appropriate options will vary throughout the life cycle of the product.

When a product is introduced into a market, companies tend to use either skimming or penetration pricing strategies. In skimming pricing strategies, products are introduced at a high price to skim off the cream of the customers who are price-insensitive. This is useful if the market is small and costs need to be recovered quickly. A rapid skimming strategy uses high price and extensive promotion to face competition and establish market share quickly. When no serious competition is expected, a slow skimming strategy may be used – high price with low promotion.

Penetration pricing strategies are used for entering large markets at a low price. This enables a company to build up a major market share quickly. Marginal pricing and experience curve effects provide long-term profit and a defence against competition.

A rapid penetration strategy uses low price and high promotion. When the market is not expected to react to promotion, a slow penetration strategy with low price and low promotion is used.

In the growth and maturity stages of the product life cycle, pricing strategies will vary according to market situations (customer reactions and price competition).

Psychological pricing strategies are immersed in the mind of the customer and what they think about prices. What are the thresholds (or price points) beyond which they are less likely to buy? How do prices affect their perceptions, attitudes, intentions and actual purchasing behaviour?

Prestige pricing, or high prices, can confirm a product's top-quality status in the mind of some buyers. A price increase can sometimes be presented as a signal of quality and cause sales to go up.

Differential pricing strategies set different prices for different market segments. This might be in the form of a geographical pricing strategy or regional pricing, with different prices charged in different areas.

Product line pricing is another strategy used for lines of products or services, with prices stepping up from a basic standard product as options and extras are added to the product. This price lining is typical of many consumer brands.

Finally, research reveals that most companies do not consider in detail all of these alternative pricing strategies throughout the life of a product or brand, despite the fact that the final price strategy directly affects long-term profitability and market share.

Pricing strategies can be defensive or aggressive, options will vary throughout the life cycle

If a product retails at £9.99, what price can a manufacturer charge?

The 3Cs – cost, competitors and customers – obviously affect prices. There is a section devoted to each of them on pages 179–84.

But there are many other factors worthy of mention when it comes to setting prices. Channels of distribution, exchange rates, legal constraints, raw material costs, inflation, trade embargoes, the terms of sale, non-monetary pricing and more affect prices.

Take distribution. If a manufacturer wants its product to sell through retail stores at say, £9.99, it cannot sell into the retail store at more than £4.00. Here, a multiple of 2.5 is used to allow for the retailer's required margin and any taxes such as VAT. This multiple varies in different markets.

To make it more complicated some retail chains insist on buying through third party distributors. This means the multiple could go from 2.5 up to 3 to allow for the distributor's margins. The manufacturer's maximum price is cut from £4.00 to £3.33.

Also, overseas distribution has the added complication of larger transport costs and fluctuating exchange rates. Swinging exchange rates make life difficult when selling into international markets. In one year alone, the US$ exchange rate swung from $2.00 to $1.50 against the £, so immediately cutting revenues by 25 per cent and profits by even more. Customers don't care about exchange rates, they only care about the price they see.

Some markets are not allowed to move their prices up and down as they please. Industry watchdogs, or regulatory bodies, are created to monitor prices and ensure that they are not raised beyond a certain reasonable level. And, of course, raw material costs have a direct impact on total costs.

Organizational markets seem to be more sympathetic to the need to increase prices as a result of increased raw materials costs than consumer markets, where buyers don't care about the details of increased raw material costs.

Inflation is a problem. Prices are affected by inflation as it increases raw material costs and reduces the market's spending power. Imagine being a marketing manager in Russia back in 1994 when a hyperinflation spasm occurred. In one day the rouble lost 25 per cent of its value. Shopkeepers shut their premises to mark up prices as the currency slumped. Queues formed at petrol stations as drivers attempted to buy petrol before prices moved up.

In the US, petrol stations give discounts for cash. Other markets have other discounts such as 'early order' and 'bulk order' discounts. And payment can sometimes be non-monetary as in the case of trade-ins, barter and strategic alliances.

The terms of sale, inflation, raw material costs, regulatory bodies and distribution channels, along with the 3Cs, are just some of the factors which make setting prices a fascinating challenge.

A manufacturer's prices can be multiplied by 2.5 to allow for retailers margins, delivery and taxes

What are Ohmae's 3Cs which influence pricing?

The 3Cs – costs, competitors and customers – are integrated and affect pricing. They have a profound influence on prices. Here is Kenichi Ohmae[2] talking about the 3Cs.

> 'In the real world he or she may pay the price that you wish or your company can make money and in most cases they would not want to pay that much money that you charge. So if you did not have a competition you can just claim that this is it, but in reality you have competition and in reality you have cost structure. Now in dealing with these two things, competition and cost structure of your own corporation, strategy comes in and therefore strategy is developed in conjunction with 3Cs, which is competition, customers and your corporation cost structure, and if your company develops a successful strategy that means customers want a better deal by your company than competition and it is sustainable in that your cost structure is lower, low enough to make profit on the sustained basis. That is the process of strategy. So to develop a very good strategy you have to have a very good marketing input to it because marketing could be put in perspective of customers and competition.'

So there you have it. If there was no competition you could charge what you want, that is, if customers really wanted your product or service.

In reality, there is competition that drives down prices. Meanwhile, you have costs that must not continuously rise above the market prices. So cost structures, competition and customers are all integrated key factors in setting prices.

The Three C's:

Competition
Customers
Costs

Ohmae's 3Cs

How many different types of costs are there?

Marketers need to understand costs. If you don't know your costs, how do you know if you're making a profit or a loss? How can you be sure your prices won't put you out of business? There are many different types of costs. We're going to look at five different types: fixed costs, variable costs, total costs, marginal costs and full unit costs.

Fixed costs are costs that basically remain fixed, regardless of how many units are produced and sold. They include rent and rates, management salaries, and so on. These are also called fixed overheads costs, say £10,000.

Variable costs are costs that vary directly with the number of units produced. They include raw materials and labour, say £10.00 per unit.

Fixed costs and all of the variable costs are added together to produce total cost.

Now here's the interesting bit. Here's where costs can be used to help to create some successful pricing strategies. Some organizations are experts at using this next type of cost, called marginal cost.

Armed with the knowledge of its fixed and variable costs (total cost) a firm can calculate its marginal cost. The marginal cost is the extra cost of making one extra unit. It is, for example, the difference in total costs when you produce 101 units instead of 100.

This is the basis of marginal pricing, where you look at your sales forecasts and set a price based on the lower marginal costs that you know you can achieve in the future. This enables you to set prices below competitors.

In this example, the marginal cost of one extra unit is £10.00. This happens to be the same as the variable cost. Although this is often the case, remember it is not always the case.

For example, if the extra unit takes you beyond the maximum capacity of the factory and you build an extra factory then the marginal cost would be the extra cost of the additional factory plus the additional unit variable cost.

The fifth type of cost is the full unit cost. This means allocating a proportion of the fixed overhead costs to each unit produced to get a 'full' cost. Add this proportion of the fixed costs to the unit variable cost and you will find the full unit cost.

One way of calculating it is to take the total cost (remember total cost is the fixed cost and all the variable costs), and to divide it by the number of units produced. You can see how full unit costs generally go down as production goes up.

Meanwhile, remember the five costs – fixed, variable, total, marginal and full unit costs.

The five types of cost

Why should you avoid a price war at all costs?

Beware of playing follow the leader. Particularly if the leader is a giant. It may be OK while you follow its price increases, but what happens when it starts to cut prices? Giants can usually afford to cut prices. But can you? For how long? Is this the only way to compete – on prices? Of course it's not. But it certainly is an aggressive way to compete. It requires big resources to be able to cut prices and forfeit revenues. And if it degenerates into a price war, then it becomes quite a savage affair. The strongest survive and the weak, well, they go out of business.

Here's Theodore Levitt talking about a price war in the US cigarette market. 'They cut prices, but Marlboro had sent the message, it was a declaration of war, they cut prices not to compete but to kill.'[3]

Mass production, cost efficiencies and a willingness to flex one's pricing muscles are not the only strengths an organization can have. There are many others such as better products, better reputation, better relationships with customers… So why compete on price if it is not your strength? Why compete with a weakness? Why not compete with a strength instead of a weakness? In sport, you play to your strengths and avoid your weaknesses. You pass the ball to your best players, or to the side of the pitch where your best players are. You compete where you are strong. The same applies in business. If you are not the most cost efficient, you don't compete on prices, you compete on your service or your quality. You play to your strengths.

Ask anyone to name the best product or service they know of in any category and you'll find it's rarely the cheapest. That's not to say that you can ignore competitors and their pricing. You can't. You have to be prepared to compete in different ways with price being one of many tools.

Not all customers are price sensitive. This means not all customers chase the cheapest price. Some do. Some don't. The question is, what do yours do? How many are price sensitive? What proportion will you lose if you don't match a competitor's lower prices?

It often depends on the customer's level of awareness of a competitor's offering. What proportion of your customers will hear about the competitor's price offer and what percentage of them will bother to switch? Perhaps these kind of promiscuous shoppers with zero loyalty should be avoided in the first place.

A few organizations research their target market's price sensitivity or price elasticity. Other organizations not only gauge their customers' likely reactions to price changes, they also gauge the competition's likely reaction in a grand game of chess – in business it's called game theory – in reality it's no game… competitor's prices can kill.

> **"**They cut prices…, it was a declaration of war…, they cut prices not to compete but to kill.**"**
>
> *Professor Theodore Levitt*

Price wars should be avoided

Don't all customers feel the same about prices?

Prices mean different things to different customers. To some the highest price guarantees the best quality. To others it pushes them away by building barriers – walls of exclusivity.

Other customers search for the best price. They enquire about prices. They talk to their friends about prices. And others haggle. They are prepared to hassle and negotiate. Recessions make markets 'buyers markets' when buyers realize that suppliers are desperate for their custom. The realization of this power shift gives some buyers a licence to negotiate. In markets stalls, in showrooms, even in retail stores. Other customers are brand loyal and will stick with their preferred brand regardless of any 'reasonable' changes in price.

This range of 'reasonableness' can be measured through price elasticity. This basically measures the market's sensitivity to price changes. If prices go up, do unit sales go down? By how much? And if prices go down, how much do unit sales go up?

Some customers are more price sensitive than others. Some don't care about prices at all as long as the quality is right. Others chase cheap prices, while others ignore them. Here's Sam Howe[4] from SouthWestern Bell.

'Pricing elasticity – we'll often go out and do a study, I shouldn't say too often because it is a very complicated study to undertake, and ask people in distinct cells within the research "how much would you pay for, let's say, Sky Sports?"

'Now we may do this, for instance, in regards to raising the price of Sky Sports, let's say its £3.99 a month right now, should we raise it £1.00, £2.00, £3.00? It's not a question of what you can get away with as much as what does the market determine the price to be, and you make those trade-offs between rate and volume, and it's very important because it may be in our mind that we want to get it to everybody, but on the other hand it is a good idea to price it just right. We may be willing to lose some customers for the right price, so I can tell you we will probably go up £2 on that product specifically based on some research we have done.'

So prices send different messages to different customers. Some are more price sensitive than others. Some don't care about prices at all as long as the quality is right. Others chase cheap prices and others again steer clear of low prices. The trick, it seems, is to be able to aggregate the data and decide which prices are best for which customers and then choose accordingly.

Some customers are price sensitive, others are not

Why is a cost-orientated approach to pricing wrong?

A totally cost-orientated approach to pricing is wrong, because it ignores the marketplace. Here, customers and competition are deemed irrelevant when setting prices. Prices are set according to production and delivery costs. This is classic myopic marketing, where production dictates prices while ignoring customers, their needs, wants and abilities to pay.

In the 1950s pricing was purely a financial issue. Calculate costs and then add a percentage or mark-up to set a price – a fixed formula called 'cost plus'. Rigidly applied, constant cost plus pricing can cause a company's demise as opportunities to increase prices are forfeited, and sometimes necessary price reductions are refused.

Cost plus pricing also excludes the possibility of varying prices across different regions.

On the other hand, costs cannot be ignored. Good marketers will always be aware of costs: fixed, variable, total, marginal and full unit costs. They all provide useful insights into a product or service's contribution, profitability and levels of sales required to break even. But it is the over-emphasis, and sometimes the total emphasis, on costs that ignore the market and cause inevitable problems.

One point worth mentioning is the distinction between mark-up and margin. Mark-up is the percentage added to costs to get a price. Margin, on the other hand, is calculated against the selling price instead of the cost.

For example, say the tie I am wearing costs £6.00. Operating on a cost plus of, say, 50 per cent, the selling price is…?

£9.00

£6.00 plus £3.00, which is 50 per cent of £6.00, equals £9.00. There is a £3.00 'mark-up' on the cost.

Now to calculate the margin on sale price, put the £3.00 over the selling price of £9.00 to get…?

33 per cent or one-third.

Remember this: margin on sale is always less than mark-up on cost.

Here is how they compare. The 50 per cent mark up on the smaller cost figure is the same as a 33 per cent margin on the larger sales price figure. Marketers are interested in margins and costs. Sales is one thing, margin on sales is another. Both are indicators of effectiveness of the marketing effort.

One other form of cost-orientated pricing is ROI pricing – return on investment pricing. This means that a certain profit or return is required from each investment. It is similar to cost plus and is often used for large capital goods pricing.

Finally, while a good grasp of costs is vital, prices dictated by costs can leave a company drifting far from its customers and the marketplace. The next section on market-orientated approach to pricing is worth reading now.

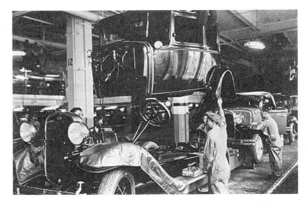

A cost-orientated approach to pricing was popular in the 1900s when prices were purely a financial issue based upon costs plus a mark-up called 'cost plus'

What is the market-orientated approach to pricing?

A market-orientated approach looks outside the organization first and inside second.

Outside means the marketplace and inside means internal costings. So looking outside brings different types of customers and competitors into view. Which kind of customers expect what kind of prices? How much are they prepared to pay? What is their threshold or limit? How do competitors' prices compare?

Price lining is a typical example, where different prices and products accommodate different types of customers using the same basic product or service.

Finding out which customers are prepared to pay what for any particular version of the same product requires research. Sadly, surprisingly few companies bother to research their prices. Recent US studies reveal that less than 15 per cent of all US companies carry out any serious pricing research.

There are, however, several ways of researching prices: in-store testing that varies prices in different stores in different regions; laboratory-based simulated test markets and multiple trade-off analysis or conjoint analysis.

Conjoint analysis allows different combinations of prices, features, benefits and brand names to be evaluated so that the marketers can identify the best marketing mix for any particular segment.

Different segments have different levels of price sensitivity. It is relatively easy to estimate market share according to different prices – if you allow for different levels of price elasticity in different segments, for example, regional markets.

Regional pricing, prestige pricing, price lining, promotional pricing, penetration pricing and psychological odd pricing are just some approaches to market-orientated pricing. Arguably the ultimate market-orientated pricing is a negotiated price? And don't forget the competition – monitoring your competitors' prices should be standard practice.

Sales representatives, trade shows, conferences and published case studies all feed information into the marketing intelligence and information system that, in turn, helps the marketer to set the right price. The section on competition (on page 181) explains the dangers of blindly following the giant's pricing strategy.

A structured, or systematic, approach to market-orientated pricing is best (see next page).

Market-orientated pricing looks outside the organization
(at the market) first and inside (at costs) second

What is the systematic approach to pricing?

There are several different approaches to developing a logical, structured approach to developing the right price. Essentially, they should all consider target market customers and competitors, marketing objectives and marketing strategies, positioning and the marketing mix, costs, margins and break-even points before considering the range of pricing options.

Eventual selection of a pricing strategy leads to a clear pricing policy that culminates in a set of prices, discounts and terms – the 'terms of trade'. And like anything else in marketing, it is all subject to review to ensure that it works.

You can probably see the SOS part of the SOSTAC approach used in marketing planning (see Chapter 3). Situation analysis, objective and strategy – first look at the market, its customers, segments, price sensitivity, ability to pay certain prices, competitor's prices and distributor's margins.

Next, look at pricing in the context of overall marketing objectives such as market share or sales. If these are aggressive objectives, like double market share, then penetration pricing might follow. On the other hand, if the marketing objective is to increase the proportion of upmarket customers then premium pricing might emerge.

On a more detailed level, prices must fit with the overall desired positioning of the brand. It's no use having premium prices if your image is cheap and nasty. Equally it's no use having cut prices if customers wrongly perceive you as expensive. So prices must fit with the marketing mix. The product quality should not contradict the pricing policy, for example, charging high prices with low-quality products.

Next come the costs. Although they should not dictate, they cannot be ignored. Cost/volume analysis helps to identify the costs at different levels of sales/production. The section on costs looks at this in more detail.

After this, several pricing strategies can be evaluated as to how well they integrate into the overall marketing objectives and strategies, sales volumes, levels of profitability, and so on. This may involve researching prices, which are discussed in the section on market-orientated pricing.

Now, and only now, are you in a position to choose a pricing strategy that guides all prices which, in turn, facilitates faster decision making and consistency of prices.

Like everything in marketing, pricing needs to be constantly monitored and changed if it proves to be a problem. Pricing is crucial. It requires special care and attention.

*A carefully structured approach rather than a high-risk game
of Russian roulette is required when setting prices*

What are the kinds of problems that relate to pricing?

Nothing in life is simple, particularly with pricing. Inflation, competition, distributors, discounts, strategic alliances, new negotiators, barter, bid prices, transfer prices and international pricing keep a myriad of problems and challenges ready to entertain marketers at any particular time.

Imagine trying to set prices in a country where 1,000 per cent rampant inflation requires hourly price changes!

The competition can change their prices at any time. Can you? Do you want to? What is your policy? Do you have one? Some retail chains insist on buying through distributors rather than directly from manufacturers. This may mean that a product with a retail price point of £1.99 may have to be sold by the manufacturer at £0.66 instead of £0.80.

Take regional pricing. It has its own special problems, particularly in the international arena. Here's Professor Peter Doyle.

'International pricing strategies are decided like this. Ideally what companies try to do is to maximize profits in each individual market. So, they estimate the price sensitivity in markets and charge higher prices in less price-sensitive markets and lower prices in more price-sensitive markets. So typically a company might charge high prices in Germany and low prices in Portugal, where competition is fiercer and consumers are less well off. The problem is though changing , and the reason why it is changing is that you're getting carry over effects. It's becoming more and more difficult to isolate markets.

'Three things are happening. First of all, you're getting the growth of parallel imports, people are shipping, wholesalers are shipping products from a low-price market to high-price markets. Secondly, communication is getting better, so that buyers are asking suppliers, "What prices are you charging elsewhere?" A big problem in the pharmaceutical company where the authorities in negotiating with pharmaceutical companies want to know what price the product is going to be in different countries, and then they want to negotiate the lowest possible price.

'I think, thirdly, that buyers are increasingly multinational (for example, Ford and General Motors), and what they are doing is they are bringing pricing together by choosing to buy from countries where prices are lower. So that pricing is getting much more complex. What it means is companies have to take a sort of much broader view on pricing.'[5]

This means that multinational organizations might like to have a simple global pricing structure, but markets and their ability to pay high prices vary particularly between northern and southern Europe or developing nations and the developed West. So a single common price is difficult to sustain. Then again, if prices do vary regionally, today's smart shopper can shop via the Internet or other networks to find the lowest price somewhere else in the world and purchase accordingly. One way round this is to try and develop local brands with appropriate prices. Although this, of course, detracts from the business benefits derived from global brands, it does offer a solution to an ever increasing global pricing problem.

So, every problem has a solution – even difficult pricing problems.

Every problem has a solution

Notes

[1]Kotler, P (1997), *Marketing Management – Analysis, Planning, Implementation and Control*, 9th edn, Prentice Hall, London.

[2]Ohmae, K (1999), Marketing CD ROM Title 8: Pricing, Multimedia Marketing Consortium, London.

[3]Levitt, T (1999), Marketing CD ROM Title 8: Pricing, Multimedia Marketing Consortium, London.

[4]Howe, S (1999) Marketing CD ROM Title 8: Pricing, Multimedia Marketing Consortium, London. You can explore the video browser in Marketing CD ROM Title 8: Pricing, Multimedia Marketing Consortium, London, to see how SouthWestern Bell research their prices to measure price sensitivity or elasticity.

[5]Doyle, P (1999) Marketing CD ROM Title 8: Pricing, Multimedia Marketing Consortium, London.

nine

distribution
decisions

- Why is dull distribution so important?
- How many different types of distribution channels are there?
- What are logistics?
- What are your distribution strategies?
- What are the distributor's responsibilities?
- Are retailers really required?
- Do you need a big salesforce?
- Is armchair shopping here to stay?
- How do you select a distribution channel?
- How do you choose a distributor?
- How do you control distributors?
- How do you motivate channel partners?

Why is dull distribution so important?

Buying a computer by mail order, petrol at a supermarket, mortgages over the phone and phones themselves from vending machines are just some innovations in distribution that create competitive advantage as customers are offered newer, faster, cheaper, safer and easier ways of buying products and services.

Without distribution even the best product or service fails. Author Jean-Jacques Lambin believes a marketer has two roles: (1) to organize exchange through distribution; and (2) to organize communication.

Physical distribution, or place, must integrate with the other Ps in the marketing mix. For example, the design of product packaging must fit on to a pallet, into a truck and on to a shelf. Prices are often determined by distribution channels and the image of the channel must fit in with the supplier's required 'positioning'. Coca-Cola make distribution and promotion work together, particularly as they see this as one of their 'core competencies'.[1]

Distribution is important because, first, it affects sales – if it's not available it can't be sold. Most customers won't wait. Second, distribution affects profits and competitiveness, as it can contribute up to 50 per cent of the final selling price of some goods. This affects cost competitiveness as well as profits, as margins are squeezed by distribution costs.

Third, delivery is seen as part of the product influencing customer satisfaction. Distribution and its associated customer service play a big part in relationship marketing.

Decisions about physical distribution are key strategic decisions. They are not short term. Increasingly they involve strategic alliances and partnerships that are founded on trust and mutual benefits. We are seeing the birth of new strategic distribution alliances where partners get access to each other's customers.[2]

Channels change throughout a product's life cycle. Changing lifestyles, aspirations and expectations, along with the IT explosion, offer new opportunities of using distribution to create a competitive edge.

Controlling the flow of products and services from producer to customer requires careful consideration. It can determine success or failure in the marketplace. The choice of channel includes choosing among and between distributors, agents, retailers, franchisees, direct marketing and a sales force.

Deciding between blanket coverage and selective distribution, vertical systems and multi-channel networks, or strategic alliances and solo sales forces requires strong strategic thinking. Logistic decisions about levels of stock, minimum order quantities, delivery methods, delivery frequency and warehouse locations have major cash-flow implications as well as customer satisfaction implications.

All of these questions are considered in more detail in the sections on channels and strategies. Meanwhile, remember Lambin – distribution is one of the two main roles of marketing.

When reflecting on Pepsi Cola's high-profile rock star ads of the 80s and 90s, Coca-Cola's chief, Roberto Goizueta, remarked:

> **"**You let me have the bottling plants and the trucks and the highly efficient systems, and I'll let you have the TV commercials. I'll beat you to a pulp over time.**"**

Without distribution, even the best product fails

How many different types of distribution channels are there?

There are many different ways of getting goods and services in front of customers. Some products go through agents, distributors and retailers before getting to the end customer – a three-level channel. Some skip the intermediaries and go directly to the end customers in a zero-level channel. And some, like Manchester United Football Club, distribute their goods through multi-channels. Here's club secretary, Ken Merrett.

> 'When it comes to sales of programmes and merchandising then there's a number of routes, obviously we have the superstore here which is open all the week and has a tremendous turnover, we have a mail order which is really going great. You can buy your programme here, you can buy it outside, you can have a subscription and you can send it anywhere in the world. We have a wholesale division apart from our retail and mail order and we stock shops anywhere so you can go in a local shop in the local precincts and they have United gear.'[3]

Now consider intermediaries such as agents, brokers, distributors, wholesalers, retailers,and so on.

Take retailers: there are many different types of retail stores, including national and international retail chains, independent stores, discount stores, department stores, superstores and more.

In consumer markets, retailing is just one way of getting goods and services to the customer. Some non-retail channels bring the store to the customer and facilitate forms of armchair shopping. These include direct mail, door-to-door selling, telesales (or telephone selling), network retailing, television shopping channels and, of course, the Internet. Then there are automated distribution points like vending machines and multimedia kiosks.

Some retailers prefer to buy through a wholesaler or distributor, who can hold stock and deliver smaller quantities exactly when and where required or 'just in time'. Other retailers prefer to buy from the producer directly. Equally, some producers prefer to skip the middlemen and deal with customers directly.

And, of course, there are new channels and new distribution opportunities emerging from strategic alliances generated through horizontal marketing systems such as SouthWestern Bell and Granada TV Shops (where Granada

TV shops offer SouthWestern Bell's cable services).[4] On top of this, technology throws open a whole new range of new possibilities for distribution.

Within the channels, there are different levels or numbers of links. In some markets, like Japan, the number of links or levels is surprisingly large.

The optimum choice of channel, or channels, changes as products and services move through their life cycles. Newspapers used to be distributed at corner stalls, then shops, doorstep delivery, supermarkets, garages, and now technology delivers it right inside your house through the Internet.

Everything changes including distribution channels. The choice of channel or channels is a critical strategic decision. The sections devoted to distribution strategies and selecting distribution channels consider these important aspects in more detail.

Everything changes including distribution channels – once newspapers were distributed at corner stalls, then shops, doorstep delivery, supermarkets, garages, and now technology delivers it right inside your house through the Internet

What are logistics?

Physically getting goods and services to customers involves many different decisions across many different activities. Many different formulae and careful calculations are required to identify the optimum order size, delivery frequency, size and number of warehouses, trucks, etc.

Physical distribution, or logistics, is one task among many other 'distribution tasks' (such as selling, servicing, promoting and collecting information). Distributing the right amount of goods to exactly the right place at exactly the right time in good condition requires lots of logistical resources including experts, information systems and equipment to move stocks.

Logistics involve a chain of events from sales forecasting to production planning to stock holding, warehousing, packing, order processing, vehicle maintenance, staffing, transporting, customer service, invoicing, and so on. In addition, dealing with returns, faulty goods, damaged goods, or the nightmare scenario of tampered goods requires the facility for reverse logistics... getting the goods back!

Planning logistics starts with customers and works backwards to production. Starting with the customer, it identifies desired delivery frequency, size and cost through to choosing the best mode of delivery, ie, plane, train, truck or ship. The optimum number of warehouses and their location and levels of stock have to be planned. Getting it all right is a complex logistical challenge.

Trade-offs have to be made between costs and service. Economic order quantities may not match customer requests. Some customers want smaller and more frequent deliveries. You must calculate what effect variations will have on sales, costs and profits in the short and long term. How does it compare to that of the competition?

Transport trade-offs also emerge. Air transport, for example, costs more than road, but because it is quicker it can: (a) reduce cash tied up with stocks in transit; (b) generate earlier customer payments resulting from earlier delivery; (c) add customer value because of quick delivery.

Speed, cost, safety and service factors affect the choice of transport mode that includes road, rail, air, water, pipeline, electronics and, occasionally, sand where in some parts of the world Coca-Cola is distributed by camel, in others by donkey.

In this new era of 'right sizing', many organizations now subcontract their marketing logistics as it requires areas of expertise that may be beyond the organization's distinctive competencies.

Here they look for strategic partners, who may be expert distribution companies or horizontal marketing systems, where different organizations share their expertise and give each other access to new customer segments.

Customers don't care who handles the logistics, whether in-house or subcontracted out. They simply want goods delivered on time, in a secure, cost-effective and, ideally, friendly way.

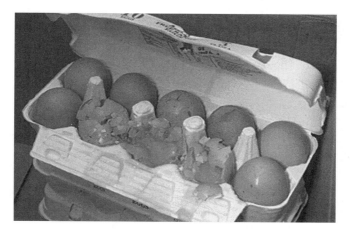

Distributing the right amount of goods to exactly the right place, at the exactly the right time in good condition, requires lots of logistical resources

What are your distribution strategies?

Distribution strategy is influenced by the market structure, the firm's objectives, its resources and, of course, its overall marketing strategy. All these factors are addressed in more detail in the section on selecting distribution channels (page 212).

The first strategic decision is whether the distribution is to be intensive (with mass distribution into all outlets as in the case of confectionery); selective (with carefully chosen distributors, eg, speciality goods such as car repair kits); or exclusive (with distribution restricted to upmarket outlets, as in the case of Gucci clothes).

The next strategic decision clarifies the number of levels within a channel such as agents, distributors, wholesalers and retailers. In some Japanese markets there are many, many intermediaries involved.

Next comes the sensitive strategic decision of whether to go single channel or multi-channel. Some producers, like Manchester United FC, use multi-channels – they use many different routes, direct and indirect, to bring their products to their customers. Multi-channel systems like this are common where intensive distribution is required. So direct marketing is combined with indirect marketing through intermediaries.

Then comes the next level of strategic decisions concerning strategic relationships and partnerships. Two common strategies are vertical marketing systems and horizontal marketing systems.

Vertical marketing systems (VMSs) involve suppliers and intermediaries working closely together instead of against each other. They plan production and delivery schedules, quality levels, promotions and sometimes prices. Resources like information, equipment and expertise are shared. The system is usually managed by a dominant member, or 'channel captain'. A VMS is more flexible than vertical integration, where the manufacturer actually owns the distribution channel; for example, Doctor Marten's boot manufacturers own their own retail store.

Horizontal marketing systems occur where organizations operating on the same channel level (eg two suppliers or two retailers) cooperate. They then share their distribution expertise and distribution channels, for example, SouthWestern Bell and Granada TV shops.[5] This can speed up the time taken to penetrate the market. There is room for creative alliances here.

Resources available affect distribution strategy. Who can handle outbound logistics, marketing, sales and servicing? Can the supplier afford to deliver small quantities, can it provide more trucks, can its sales force 'push' products into national retail chains? Can the organization deal with thousands, maybe even millions of customers – can it cope? Does it want to devote huge resources here, or would it prefer to utilize someone else's resources in return for a slice of the profits? Difficult marketing dilemmas which make distribution strategy both critical and interesting. The sections on distribution channels explore this in more detail.

> Horizontal marketing systems, strategic partnerships, marketing marriages, call them what you want… they offer a lot of room for creative thinking.

There are many innovations in distribution which create competitive advantage

What are the distributor's responsibilities?

Distributors give suppliers access to a target market, either directly to the end customer or through the distributor's own retail network.

Distributors have several other functions:

1. Break bulk – this allows the manufacturer to maintain large production runs which would be too big for the end customers.

2. Hold stock – this reduces the manufacturer's space and cash (ie, working capital) tied up in stock.

3. Give credit – to customers and therefore bear both the risk of bad debts and the cash (or working capital) tied up in debtors.

4. Deliver goods – in smaller appropriate quantities to customers.

5. Collect information – directly from the marketplace. This includes generating sales forecasts and also contributing to the manufacturer's marketing intelligence and information systems.

6. Provide a sales force – some distributors have their own sales force on the road, generating business for themselves and the manufacturers they represent.

7. Provide a promotional vehicle – by including manufacturers' products in the distributor's catalogues, mail shots, trade shows, advertisements, etc. Distributors become ambassadors for the producer.

Incidentally, agents do 5, 6 and 7 but not 1, 2, 3 or 4. Both distributors and agents need support. This may involve training, entertaining, motivating and controlling as well as providing an array of promotional materials such as brochures.

Distributors require resources like management time for visits, meetings, dinners, exhibitions, and so on. They require stocks of brochures, sales aids and financial support for marketing activities such as shared advertising or co-operative advertising, shared promotions, branch openings and trade shows. So a producer can only support a limited number of distributors.

Distributors also cost money. This means discounts – the supplier sells to the distributor at a discounted price so that the distributor can add its margin and earn its own income.

Negotiations between suppliers and distributors are not just about discounts. Today manufacturers look to develop longer-term partnerships with distributors. These strategic alliances have shared goals. They work closely together to achieve them. The choice of distributor is vital since it is expensive to swap and change after investing time, money and expertise in selecting and developing the relationship.

Problems do occur. Distributors have other product lines to worry about as well… and sometimes they belong to competitors. Equally, suppliers who use multiple channels can create 'channel conflict' when they skip the distributor and deal directly with end customers. Managing distributors demands many skills from strategic analysis to building friendly relations. The section on control (page 216) examines this in more detail.

Responsibilities	Distributor	Agent
Break Bulk	✓	X
Hold Stock	✓	X
Give Credit	✓	X
Deliver Goods	✓	X
Collect Information	✓	✓
Provide a Sales Force	✓	✓
Provide a Promotional Vehicle	✓	✓

The difference between distributors and agents

Are retailers really required?

Retailers provide suppliers with access to target markets. In some markets they decide which brand they will stock and how much shelf space each will receive. This has, in many markets, transferred power from the suppliers to the retailers. Many large retailers control sales and dictate terms. They even launch their own brands in competition with the supplier's brand.

Despite all of this, retailers are a vital channel for most consumer products. But a 'push strategy' by the supplier is not enough. It's no good trying just to sell in or push stocks into a retailer, even though this requires good products and great sales skills. Retailers demand a 'pull strategy' to support the push. They are interested in the size of the supplier's advertising budget, which will get customers 'pulling' the stock through the channel by taking products off the retailers' shelves.

Many of the large retail chains buy directly from suppliers. While the smaller, independent retailers buy through an intermediary such as a full service wholesaler or a cash 'n' carry.

There are many types of retail store – from upmarket department stores, to mass market discount stores, department stores, specialist stores, and so on.

In addition to merchandising and display, the retailer's skills also involve selecting store sites, merchandising and managing stock levels precisely. This requires accurate information systems.

Large retail chains collect information and monitor exactly which products are selling in which stores in which parts of the world – how sales respond to advertising, what promotions work best, and so on. In fact, data collected at the cash register through electronic point-of-sale (EPOS) systems simultaneously update stock records, trigger requests for stock from the warehouse and even update the suppliers so that they can prepare 'just in time' deliveries for the following day.

So retailers become strategic partners in the distribution chain. Manufacturers and major retailers work closely together, creating vertical marketing systems – planning deliveries, production runs, quality control and sometimes even product design. They also plan merchandising, space allocation and lay-out, cooperative advertising and joint promotions.

Suppliers obviously prefer to get the prime shelf space at eye level and the ends of gondolas. Distribution arrangements come right down to space allocation. Where exactly will the product be displayed? How much space will it be allocated? How many shelf facings will it get? What other products will be beside it? All of these affect sales, so they are negotiated carefully.

Many manufacturers use multiple channels. They sell and distribute to customers both directly and indirectly through vending machines, distributors and independent retailers as well as the traditional big retail chains.

Retailers can become strategic partners planning joint promotions, space allocation and information in pursuit of the 'illusive customer'

Do you need a big salesforce?

Many organizations do not include the cost of their sales force in their marketing communications budget because they see the sales force as part of distribution – a way of getting products and services to customers.

The size of the sales force affects sales. Increase the sales force and you increase distribution penetration, which subsequently increases sales because more customers get access to the product. But one sales person can only cover so much. If there were 2,000 potential customers and one sales representative could only make four calls a day – how many sales reps would you need?

Well one rep could make 20 calls a week and with 50 working weeks, one rep could make 1,000 calls a year. Therefore two reps would be required, that is, if neither rep got sick, took holidays, and both stayed on the road out of the office for the whole year. It also assumes that each customer only needs one visit a year. If each customer needed one visit a month then suddenly 24 hardworking, healthy reps would be required.

In reality, big customers require a lot of attention. Some sales reps may spend all year trying to win just one or two of these as well as several smaller ones. This kind of sales rep is an 'order getter' and likes to go after new business. Other reps prefer to be 'order takers', maintaining and servicing existing customers.

In most cases, the sales force is used to create a network of distributors. In other cases it sells to end users. Avon cosmetics, for example, sells directly to millions of homes around the world.

Selection, training, motivation and control are all important components of any successful sales force. If all these are managed properly and the product is worthy, then the probability of success increases.

Some organizations prefer to use their own sales force, others will only keep a small sales force that sells into a network of distributors and agents, who then sell the product through their own, larger sales force network.

Other organizations look for strategic partnerships involving horizontal systems, where sales and distribution may be handled by the partner's sales force.

As full-time sales forces are so expensive, some organizations hire contract sales forces or a 'field marketing' agency, which supplies a temporary sales team for a fixed period of time, typically during seasonal peaks and during special promotions.

One aspect of selling that is never subcontracted out is selling to key customers such as major accounts. This is the responsibility of the marketing or sales director.

Successful selling is fundamental to successful distribution which, in turn, is one of the marketer's key tasks.

One aspect of selling that must never be subcontracted out is selling to key customers. In fact, some companies insist that all board members take responsibility for at least one major customer (after being trained)

Is armchair shopping here to stay?

Direct marketing gives an organization access to the target market without any intermediaries. The customer is sold to inside their own home or office. And delivery follows, directly into the home or the office. This is 'armchair shopping' as customers do not have to go out, shop and traipse wearily home again. For example, pizza companies are among many who offer home sales and home delivery to facilitate today's growing army of busy people. Even computers and computer peripherals are bought and delivered through the post.

Some manufacturers do their own direct marketing so that they gain direct access to the market. Some intermediaries, such as retailers, do their own direct marketing through customer loyalty schemes and catalogues.

The purpose of direct marketing is to develop a database of customers and establish lifelong, personal relationships that generate a profitable revenue stream. They are recruited through integrated communications, such as mass media campaigns, with response mechanisms like coupons and free-phone numbers as well as sales promotions, competition entry forms, guarantee forms, Internet Web site entry forms and neighbour-get-neighbour campaigns. Telesales and mail shots from lists of prospects are also used to boost direct sales and to gather names of customers for the database.

Other forms of direct marketing include door-to-door selling, direct response TV, TV-shopping channels, the Internet and CD catalogues.

Direct marketing gives access to end customers directly, but it does require resources or at least partners with resources. For example, sophisticated databases and expert logistical systems are required if dealing with thousands or sometimes millions of customers. Getting the right goods to the right customer on time and in good condition requires expertise. Many organizations subcontract the physical distribution aspect out to 'fulfilment houses', which specialize in the logistics of stock holding, order processing, packing, despatch and invoicing.

As mentioned previously, direct marketing can cause some channel conflict particularly when, say, a manufacturer is seen to reach over the shoulder of the middleman and offer goods directly to the end customer.

Although multiple channels, or multi-channels, give a supplier more distribution options and probably better distribution penetration, they need to be handled sensitively as it can upset distributors who see direct marketing competing with them for their own customers.

Having said that, direct marketing can deliver more than increased sales and improved distribution penetration. It can deliver a database of customers, their profiles, buying behaviour and more. This is a valuable asset that is not shown on most balance sheets, but nevertheless it can have an immense impact on distribution, sales and profits in the short, medium and long term.

Armchair shopping is continuing to develop

How do you select a distribution channel?

What is the best distribution channel? How should a product or service get to the marketplace?

Do you use agents, distributors, retailers or go direct? Hold your own stock and use your own sales force, or an agency's sales force? Or perhaps tie in with a distributor who will hold stock, handle deliveries and use its sales force to do the selling? Or just sell into a retail chain and let them do the rest? You have to get to your customers. Be where they are. Be available.

The strategic choice of distribution channel is influenced by market structure, the firm's objectives, the resources available and the overall marketing strategy.

Firstly, the market structure. It starts with customers and the product or service itself. Where do they buy and consume it? Are customers concentrated in one area? Do they need to see it and test it before buying? Do they want to buy directly or indirectly through intermediaries? Remember, the number of intermediaries in the channel affects prices as each middleman adds a margin on to the final price. Too many middlemen can push the final price beyond the reach of the target market. You can see Professor Doyle explain why the viability of the middleman is determined by margins and number of customers in the linker in Marketing CD ROM Title 9.

Secondly, some channels achieve sales, market share and profit objectives better than others. The potential for repeat sales also influences the choice of channel.

Thirdly, resources. Some channels will require more resources than others. Can the supplier afford to employ its own sales force, or will a lower cost network of distributors and agents do the job as well? Remember, the sales force is a fixed overhead, while discounts to distributors and commissions to agents are variable costs. Middlemen cost money. So is it better to give, say, 30 per cent discount to a distributor or spend it on direct marketing activities instead?

Finally, it all comes back to the overall marketing strategy in order to meet the marketing objectives. The distribution channel strategy must fit in with, for example, sales objectives and positioning strategy.

Check each channel for:

- Penetration level – what percentage of the target market is covered? Sales – forecast sales levels.

- Cost – what does it cost – margins/discounts; investment in stock and vehicles; marketing costs and sales force costs?

- Other resources – what other resources are required? Management time, distributor training, cooperative advertising and exchange of information.

- Profitability of each channel.

- Customer control – do you lose control of your product or prices with some channels?

The choice of channel is an important strategic decision. It is followed by the choice of particular channel members (eg, particular distributors), see next page.

Some products like medicine, alcohol and cigarettes have to have safe distribution channels to ensure they do not end up with the wrong type of customer

How do you choose a distributor?

Having decided to go through intermediaries, the next question is whether to use agents or distributors and also how many. Unlike distributors, agents don't hold stocks – they only act as sales agents finding customers, collecting orders and passing them on to the supplier in return for a percentage commission.

How would you select a distributor or an agent? Here are some criteria:

1. Market coverage:
   Does the profile of existing customers match your target market profile?
   Is the number of customers big enough to meet the required distribution penetration?
   Is the existing sales force big enough to cover the territory?
   Are they dependent on a single individual?
   Are the existing delivery fleet and warehouse facilities adequate?

2. Sales forecast:
   How many can they sell? What are their forecasts based upon? Do they give a 'best, worst and average' forecast?
   Will they invest in large stock commitment?
   Do they have budgets to run promotions? Some suppliers ask their distributors for a marketing plan detailing how they will market the supplier's products.

3. Cost:
   What will it cost in terms of discounts, commissions, stock investment and marketing support?

4. Other Resources:
   Does the target market require anything special such as technical advice, installation, quick deliveries, instant availability? If so, can the distributor provide it?

5. Profitability:
   How much profit will the distributor generate for the supplier?

6. Control:
   Do they have a reporting system in place? How do they deal with problems? How often are review meetings scheduled? Can you influence the way they present your products?

7. Motivation:

   Does the agent or distributor convey a sense of excitement and enthusiasm about the product? What about its sales force – what's their reaction?

8. Reputation:

   Has it got a good track record? This includes the number of years in business, growth and profit record, solvency, general stability and overall reliability. Is it dependent on one key player?

9. Competition:

   Do they distribute any competitors' products?

10. Contracts:

    Some distributors demand exclusivity. Some agreements tie the supplier in for certain periods of time. Check for flexibility in case things go wrong.

The bottom line is: can the agent or distributor be motivated, controlled and trusted? Motivated to sell your product among a range of others, controlled to feed back results or change strategy if requested… and trusted to act as a reliable ambassador of your product?

Distributor Selection Criteria	Score
1. Market coverage	
2. Sales forecast	
3. Cost	
4. Other resources	
5. Profitability	
6. Control	
7. Motivation	
8. Reputation	
9. Competition	
10. Contracts.	

A checklist for distribution selection

How do you control distributors?

Problems in any one link in the channel can disrupt or destroy the whole distribution process when customers find goods are unknown, unavailable, delivered late or delivered damaged. And in some cases, suppliers like medical companies, cigarette companies and football clubs have to ensure their products are not distributed to the wrong customer.

Suppliers like to have some control of their products throughout the distribution process. They need to watch all the links in the chain. The closer a supplier works with an intermediary the greater the chance of success. In vertical marketing systems they work closely together sharing data, facilities and finances. Cooperation replaces confrontation. Both parties have to help each other constantly to improve.

Having said that, how does the marketing manager know whether it is working in the first place? Goodwill alone is not enough. Good partnerships establish measurement criteria early on. Regular reviews then help managers to manage (or control). They even agree a forum for dealing with problems, disagreements and conflicts when they inevitably occur. Having said that, suppliers may have to drop a channel member if it continually underperforms despite attempts to resolve problems. Performance criteria must be clearly defined early on and measured regularly. What are the typical performance criteria?

Monthly, quarterly and yearly sales quotas are easily measured, as are average stock levels, average delivery times, number of returns or damaged goods, customer service and level of marketing support.

Customer service can be measured by mystery shoppers who report back directly to the manufacturer. It can also be gauged by actual visits to a distributor's customers and asking them what they think of the service. Marketing support can be measured by checking exhibitions, catalogues and sales promotions.

Distributors and agents can also collect useful information which can be fed into the supplier's marketing information and intelligence system. Quality of information may vary. Some distributors don't want to exchange information with suppliers and it is as well to make arrangements in advance.

Personal visits reveal a certain amount of information such as level of interest and motivation that the distributor or agent expresses. Intermediaries have other lines to worry about and the supplier must be aware of this. This kind of information can help the supplier to choose which intermediaries should be focused upon and which dropped. There is a limit to the number of distributors or agents that, first, can be supported and, second, that are necessary to satisfy the market.

Maintaining motivation and particularly 'mindshare' is important. The section on motivation looks at this in more detail.

Suppliers need to watch all the links in the distribution chain all the time

How do you motivate channel partners?

Imagine these three scenarios. You are a producer of 'Grand Pens' a brand of fountain pens.

- A customer seeks advice from a pen shop on which pen to buy and the retailer strongly recommends yours.
- A customer asks a retailer who stocks your pen for another brand called 'Bad Pens'. The retailer recommends and offers your pen as superior.
- A retailer actively solicits business for you by asking customers buying other products to come and have a look at the exquisite 'Grand Pen'.

This retailer is obviously very motivated. 'Mindshare', as it is called in the USA, has to do with how important your product is in the distributor's mind relative to the other lines they carry. Winning the battle for the distributor's share of mind can be more important than many other marketing strategies. It applies to industrial markets and consumer markets where intermediaries play important roles in the distribution channel.

In reality, maintaining continually high levels of motivation among intermediaries presents a challenge. It requires a reasonable quality product, creative promotions, product training, joint visits between producer and distributor, cooperative advertising, merchandising and display.

Most of these apply to agents as much as to distributors and retailers. Keeping the intermediary stimulated is important. Positive motivators, like sales contests, are preferred to negative motivators, like sanctions such as reduced discounts and the threat of terminating the relationship.

A positive reward works better than a negative punishment. Ideally there should be a shared sense of responsibility... a partnership... a strategic partnership. The supplier and intermediary are there to help each other. Vertical marketing systems are a good example.

Clear communications covering sales goals, review meetings, reporting procedures, marketing strategy, training, market information required, and suggestions for improvements all help. Regular contact through visits, review meetings, dinners, competitions, newsletters, thank-you letters and congratulatory awards all help to keep everyone working closely together.

These are all non-financial incentives that provide a form of psychic income as opposed to financial income. That's not to say that financial incentives aren't useful motivators, it just means that there are other motivators there, too. In fact, the money spent on financial incentives is often spent more effectively when the sales person is rewarded with a plaque, a gold pen or a holiday in the Bahamas rather than just the cash which tends to get soaked up and lost in a sea of ordinary household daily expenditure. Non-cash rewards appeal to the higher levels of Maslow's hierarchy of needs... belonging, esteem and self-actualization.

Despite this, conflict can occur when too many distributors are appointed within close proximity to each other, or the producer engages in a multiple channel strategy of direct marketing as well as marketing through intermediaries. Carefully motivating distributors is vital if goods are to flow smoothly through the channel and reach satisfied customers.

Positive rewards can motivate channel partners to go to extraordinary lengths to help your company

Notes

[1]You can see how Coca-Cola further integrate the timing of distribution and promotion in the Hall Of Fame in Marketing CD ROM Title 9: Distribution Decisions, Multimedia Marketing Consortium, London.

[2]You can see SouthWestern Bell in the Hall Of Fame in Marketing CD ROM Title 9: Distribution Decisions (Multimedia Marketing Consortium, London) explain how marketing marriages provide new ways of getting products and services in front of customers.

[3]You can see more of Manchester United FC in Marketing CD ROM Title 9: Distribution Decisions, Multimedia Marketing Consortium, London.

[4]You can see Sam Howe, SouthWestern Bell discussing horizontal marketing systems in the video browser in Marketing CD ROM, Title 9: Distribution Decisions, Multimedia Marketing Consortium, London.

[5]Ibid.

integrated
marketing
communications

- ➡ What is integrated marketing communications (IMC)?
- ➡ How does IMC help your company?
- ➡ Who or what will try to stop me from integrating my communications?
- ➡ How do customers process information?
- ➡ What are 1–2–1 tools and how do they naturally integrate?
- ➡ How do advertising, PR and sponsorship integrate?
- ➡ How do merchandising, point-of-sale, packaging and exhibitions integrate naturally?
- ➡ How can sales promotions add extra value?
- ➡ What is the difference between corporate image and corporate identity?
- ➡ How does the Internet integrate?
- ➡ What are IMC's 10 golden rules?

What is integrated marketing communications (IMC)?

Integrated marketing communications is a simple concept. It ensures that all forms of communications and messages are carefully linked together. At its most basic level, integrated marketing communications, or IMC as we'll call it, means integrating all the promotional tools so that they work together in harmony.

Promotion is one of the Ps in the marketing mix. Promotion has its own mix of communications tools which include: selling, direct mail, advertising, public relations, sponsorship, exhibitions, point-of-sale, packaging, sales promotions, corporate identity and new tools like the Internet. You can explore all of these along with their different dimensions later. One other extremely powerful communications tool is word of mouth. This can be generated through employees, customer service, product quality and through other communications tools like provocative advertising, sensational sales promotions and newsworthy publicity stunts. And today, the word of mouth process can be accelerated through the Internet.

All of these communications tools work better if they work together in harmony rather than in isolation. Their sum is greater than their parts – providing they speak consistently with one voice all the time, every time.

This is enhanced when integration goes beyond just the basic communications tools. There are other levels of integration such as horizontal, vertical, internal, external and data integration.

This is how they help to strengthen integrated communications. Horizontal integration occurs across the marketing mix and across business functions – for example, production, finance, distribution and communications should work together and be conscious that their decisions and actions send messages to customers. Also different departments such as sales, direct mail and advertising can help each other through data integration. This requires a marketing information system which collects and shares relevant data across different departments. Vertical integration means marketing and communications objectives must support the higher level corporate objectives and corporate missions.[1] Meanwhile, internal integration requires internal marketing – keeping all staff informed and motivated about any new developments, from new advertisements to new corporate identities, new service standards, new strategic partners, and so on. External integration, on the other hand, requires external partners such as advertising and PR agencies to work closely together to deliver a single seamless solution – a cohesive message – an integrated message.

The many benefits of IMC are explored on the next page in the section called 'How does IMC help your company?'

Horizontal integration occurs across the marketing mix and across business functions – for example, production, finance, distribution and communications all work together to promote the brand

How does IMC help your company?

Although integrated marketing communication requires a lot of effort it delivers many benefits. It can create competitive advantage and boost sales and profits, while saving money, time and stress.

IMC wraps communications around customers and helps them to move through the various stages of the buying process. The organization simultaneously consolidates its image, develops a dialogue and nurtures its relationship with customers. This relationship marketing cements a bond of loyalty with customers that can protect them, in the long term, from the inevitable onslaught of competition. Peter Doyle suggests that this means finding new ways to delight the customer, finding new sources of value to keep a customer loyal to you.[2] The ability to keep a customer for life is a powerful competitive advantage.

IMC also increases profits through increased effectiveness. At its most basic level, a unified message has more impact than a disjointed myriad of messages. In a busy world, a consistent, consolidated and crystal clear message has a better chance of cutting through the 'noise' of over 500 commercial messages that bombard customers each and every day.

At another level, initial research suggests that images shared in advertising and direct mail boost both advertising awareness and mail shot responses. So IMC can boost sales by stretching messages across several communications tools to create more avenues for customers to become aware, aroused and ultimately to make a purchase.

Carefully linked messages also help buyers by giving timely reminders, updated information and special offers that, when presented in a planned sequence, help them to move comfortably through the stages of their buying process... and this reduces their 'misery of choice' in a complex and busy world.

IMC also makes messages more consistent and therefore more credible. This reduces risk in the mind of the buyer, which, in turn, shortens the search process and helps to dictate the outcome of brand comparisons.

Unintegrated communications send disjointed messages which dilute the impact of the message. This may also confuse, frustrate and arouse anxiety in customers. On the other hand, integrated communications present a reassuring sense of order. Consistent images and relevant, useful messages help to nurture long-term relationships with customers. Here, customer databases can identify precisely which customers need what information when… and throughout their whole buying lives.[3]

Finally, IMC saves money as it eliminates duplication in areas such as graphics and photography as they can be shared and used in, say, advertising, exhibitions and sales literature. Agency fees are reduced by using a single agency for all communications. And even if there are several agencies, time is saved when meetings bring all the agencies together – for briefings, creative sessions and tactical or strategic planning. This reduces workload and subsequent stress levels… one of the many benefits of IMC.

Time pressure reduces when agencies come together for briefs, creative, tactical and strategic meetings

Who or what will try to stop me from integrating my communications?

Despite its many benefits, integrated marketing communications has many barriers.

In addition to the usual resistance to change and the special problems of communicating with a wide variety of target audiences, there are many other obstacles which restrict IMC. These include: functional silos; stifled creativity; timescale conflicts and a lack of management know-how. Take functional silos. Rigid organizational structures are infested with managers who protect both their budgets and their power base. Sadly, some organizational structures isolate communications, data and even managers from each other. For example, the PR department often doesn't report to marketing. The sales force rarely meets the advertising or sales promotion people, and so on. Imagine what can happen when sales reps are not told about a new promotional offer! And all of this can be aggravated by turf wars or internal power battles, where specific managers resist having some of their decisions (and budgets) determined or even influenced by someone from another department.

Here are two difficult questions. What should a truly integrated marketing department look like? And how will it affect creativity? It shouldn't matter whose creative idea it is, but often it does. An advertising agency may not be so enthusiastic about developing a creative idea generated by, say, a PR or a direct marketing consultant. IMC can restrict creativity. No more wild and wacky sales promotions unless they fit into the overall marketing communications strategy. The joy of rampant creativity may be stifled, but the creative challenge may be greater and ultimately more satisfying when operating within a tighter, integrated and creative brief.

Add different timescales into a creative brief and you'll see time horizons provide one more barrier to IMC. For example, image advertising designed to nurture the brand over the longer term may conflict with shorter-term advertising or sales promotions designed to boost quarterly sales. However, the two objectives can be accommodated within an overall IMC if carefully planned.

But this kind of planning is not common. A survey back in the mid-90s revealed that most managers lack expertise in IMC. But it's not just managers, it's also agencies. There is a proliferation of single-discipline agencies. There appear to be very few people who have real experience of all the marketing communications disciplines. This lack of know-how is then compounded by a lack of commitment. The section on the golden rules for IMC examines this in more detail.

For now, understanding the barriers is the first step in successfully implementing IMC.

*Whose budget and whose idea? Just two of many sensitive
IMC problems that need to be addressed*

How do customers process information?

How do we communicate? How do customers process information? There are many models and theories. Let's take a brief look at some of them.

Simple communications models show a sender sending a message to a receiver who receives and understands it. Real life is less simple – many messages are misunderstood, fail to arrive or are simply ignored. Marketers need to have a thorough understanding of the audience's needs, emotions, interests and activities and it is essential to ensure the accuracy and relevance of any message. Instead of loud 'buy now' advertisements, many messages are often designed or 'encoded' so that the hard-sell becomes a more subtle soft-sell. The sender creates or encodes the message in a form that can be easily understood or decoded by the receiver.

Clever encoding also helps a message to cut through the clutter of other advertisements and distractions, which is called 'noise'. If successful, the audience will spot the message and then decode or interpret it correctly. The marketer then looks for 'feedback', such as coupons returned from mailshots, to see if the audience has decoded the message correctly.

The single-step model – with a receiver getting a message directly from a sender – is not a complete explanation. Many messages are received indirectly through a friend or through an opinion leader.

Communications are in fact multifaceted, multi-step and multi-directional. Opinion leaders talk to each other. Customers talk to opinion leaders and they talk to each other.

Add in 'encode, decode, noise and feedback' and the process appears more complex still.

Understanding multi-phase communications helps marketers to communicate directly through mass media and indirectly through targeting opinion leaders, opinion formers, style leaders, innovators and other influential people.

How messages are selected and processed within the minds of the target market is a vast and complex question. Although it is over 70 years old, rather simplistic and too hierarchical, a message model like AIDA attempts to map the mental processes through which a buyer passes en route to making a purchase. Here's Peter Doyle, 'But models such as AIDA do remind marketeers that on the whole, for most products, customers do go through certain stages'.[4]

There are many other models that attempt to identify each stage. In reality, the process is not always a linear sequence. Buyers often loop backwards at various stages perhaps for more information. There are other much more complex models that attempt to map the inner workings of the mind.

In reality, marketers have to select communications tools that are most suitable for the stage that the target audience has reached. For example, advertising may be very good at raising awareness or developing interest, while free samples and sales promotions may be the way to generate trial.

This is just a glimpse into some of the theory. Serious marketers read a lot more.

You must identify all the opinion formers and opinion leaders in your marketplace and work with them

AIDA = ATTENTION → INTEREST → DESIRE → ACTION

What are 1–2–1 tools and how do they naturally integrate?

Unlike mass advertising, one-to-one communication allows one person to communicate with another person directly. This is done primarily through the sales force, whether engaged in face-to-face selling or telesales. Direct mail, when an organization sends personalized letters to named individuals, is also sometimes referred to as 1–2–1 marketing.

All 1–2–1 communications, must be integrated at different levels. Firstly, information. Enquiries or leads generated from mailshots, advertisements and exhibitions are checked by a telesales team to rank the size and timing of any possible purchases. These are prioritized and the best leads, or the hottest prospects, are passed on to the sales force who then have a 1–2–1 meeting with the prospect.

Secondly, integration has to occur internally among different departments. For example, the sales force (and other staff) need to be informed of any new advertising campaigns, mailshots or promotional offers that are about to be launched. Otherwise they feel alienated and also appear ignorant if customers ask questions. All staff should be informed of any new USP (unique selling proposition) discovered by, say, the advertising agency during a 'product interrogation'. When armed with all the up-to-date information the sales people are equipped to 'close sales' or take orders.

Integrating sales promotions with the sales team also helps. For example, closing the sale becomes easier if there is an incentive on offer. This also applies to direct mail – whether generating enquiries or closing sales, it becomes easier if the target customer is offered a relevant incentive. It doesn't have to be a free Rolls Royce. Less expensive, but more relevant incentives can be very cost effective.

Going back to the sales force, they should collect relevant information to feed back into the customer database. To do this they have to be trained and motivated. All part of the sales manager's task of recruitment, training and motivation.

Some 1–2–1 sales can be completed over the phone; others require a visit; or several visits – depending on the product and customers. Marketers have to balance field sales and telesales carefully.

A different form of 1–2–1 communication occurs with word of mouth. Neighbours talk to each other and shoppers exchange opinions. It can also be initiated by NGN (neighbour-get-neighbour) campaigns, where incentives are offered if customers introduce a neighbour or a friend.

Positive word of mouth is generated by having good products, interesting promotions and exciting advertisements. 1–2–1 communications can close the final stages of the buying process. Other tools, like advertising, are generally more effective in developing the earlier stages such as spreading awareness. Needless to say 1–2–1 communications must integrate with all the communications tools.

> Welcome complaints: Only 1 in 24 dissatisfied customers bother to complain. The rest just hate you and tell their friends. And meanwhile you just keep plugging away without any alarm bells unless, of course, you're lucky enough to get a complaint.

1–2–1 communication allows one person to communicate with another directly through selling, telephone selling or direct mail

How do advertising, PR and sponsorship integrate?

Two-dimensional communications refer to advertising, publicity and sponsorship. The exposure generated by these tools is usually delivered into two dimensions.

Take advertising. Images are generally presented on two dimensions or two planes – length and breadth. For example, press and poster advertisements are generally two-dimensional, flat-page graphics. There are of course exceptions such as 3-D posters, 3-D TV and 3-D cinema.

Despite its limited dimensions, advertising can grab attention, create awareness and change attitudes among large audiences within relatively short periods of time. It informs, persuades and reminds. It also helps to build a brand's personality. It can arouse emotions and create an atmosphere that allows other communications tools, like sales promotions and the sales force, to sell at a later stage. A specialist type of advertising, called direct-response advertising, can make people act – call freephone numbers, mail enquiry coupons or even place orders.

Advertising's power to shape perceptions, thoughts and emotions is best used as part of an effective IMC programme. On its own, advertising rarely works. It has to be integrated with other communications tools – sales force, telesales team, in-store merchandise and display. For example, advertising should be integrated with PR. Like new products, new advertisements and new sales promotions may be unveiled at a press conference, thereby generating free exposure for the advertising. Some PR people even get the film of the 'making of the ad' on to television. Others get a video news release of the advertisement into television news.

Free media coverage has less resistance and higher message credibility, as audiences consider the material to be created by neutral journalists and not PR people. Publicity, however, is not controllable. Unlike advertising, the intended message can be changed completely by an editor. Other PR activities are about influencing key opinion formers and gathering third-party endorsements.

Sponsorship, sometimes comes under PR. It is a potentially powerful tool for image enhancement, increasing credibility, awareness and many other functions. Like PR, it has its risks. Media coverage is not controllable... unlike advertising.

Advertising, sponsorship and public relations can combine to increase awareness, change attitudes and start to move the customer through the stages of the buying process. Then the 2-D tools combine with 3-D, 4-D , 5-D, M-D (pages 234–41) and 1–2–1 tools to move customers comfortably through their buying process again and again.

Develop credibility before raising visibility (through advertising, PR and sponsorship).

Some PR people even get 'the making of the ad' onto television – generating free media coverage

How do merchandising, point-of-sale, packaging and exhibitions integrate naturally?

Three-dimensional communications tools have length, breadth and depth. In a sense, the audience can take hold of, step inside or physically interact with the actual communications, for example, packaging, point-of-sale, merchandising and exhibitions.

Consider packaging. It has to protect, offer convenience and communicate. The pack has been described as the 'silent salesman' in a classic book on packaging design. It has to grab attention, attract interest, deliver detailed information and ultimately make the sale. A complicated communications challenge for a simple pack.

Pack designers blend shape, size, colour, graphics and materials together to create a three-dimensional advertisement on the shelf.

Packs can trigger and arouse previously stored advertising images so that buyers recall, at least for a moment, those happy jingles and lifestyle aspirations conjured up in the advertisements. Integration occurs at a basic level when close-ups of the pack, known as 'pack shots', are used in advertisements. Advertising images can also be integrated into the packaging and point-of-sale.

Although some point-of-sale has only two dimensions such as signs and posters, most is three-dimensional. Whether it is a tailored display rack, a dump bin, bobble card, bottle collar or something more inventive, the point-of-sale offers a last chance to grab a customer. Who knows what goes through a customer's mind during the last 30 seconds before a purchase? We do know it can be influenced by a clever piece of point-of-sale.

Needless to say, packaging and point-of-sale have to integrate. Imagine if the packs didn't fit into the display rack or the colours clashed? Equally, on-pack sales promotions obviously have implications for the display, shelf space and distribution process. This means the sales force has to be aware of and sell the idea to the retail outlets. Good sales literature helps this to happen.

Investing in a high level of three-dimensional design skills for merchandising and display can be worthwhile, particularly if it is integrated with other communications tools.

Finally, exhibitions… a mini market with buyers, sellers and competitors all under one roof. Exhibitions increasingly use sophisticated 3-D designs to attract, engage and win customers.

Needless to say, successful exhibitions are fully integrated. Advertising, direct mail and the sales force invite key customers and prospects to visit the stand. Sales promotions and gifts offer incentives to visit. Copious amounts of sales literature must be available to the sales staff, who have to be fully briefed, before, during and after the show.

Exhibition stands also offer PR people publicity opportunities for both internal newsletters and external press coverage. And, of course, good stand design does more than win awards, it helps to get sales. Just one stage in the continual integration of marketing communications processes.

Exhibitions integrate with direct mail,
advertising, salesforce and of course PR

How can sales promotions add extra value?

Sales promotions present an extra dimension – the additional value not normally present in the product offering.

How about two holes of golf with Jack Nicklaus accompanied by an 80-piece orchestra playing the tune of your choice, or a Caribbean holiday or a trip to the moon? The stuff of dreams... tailoring creative sales promotion competitions to meet the fantasies of a specific target market. Promotions can also take the shape of vouchers, coupons, samples and even discounts.

Ideally, the promotion should add value to the brand and strengthen its bond with the customer. Some promotions, sadly, dilute the brand. Price promotions, for example, can damage brand image, particularly if it is positioned as an upmarket premium brand... a classic disjointed and destructive piece of unintegrated marketing communication. On the other hand, gifts, prizes and collector items which are linked to the brand can add value and strengthen the brand. Guinness, for example, uses gifts which relate to, promote and reinforce the brand. Whether a T-shirt or a toucan, each of them supports the brand's heritage. They even have 'win your own Irish pub' competitions, which associate the 'images of good quality drink' and 'Irish-ness' with the brand equity.

Sales promotions must integrate with the overall positioning of the brand.

Some estimates, which include price promotions, coupons and discounts, suggest that in many markets more money is now spent on sales promotions than on advertising. But, like advertising, how much of it is wasted? How many customers would have bought the brand anyway – whether it had a free gift or not? How many are promiscuous shoppers who have no loyalty and buy only whenever and wherever there is a 'free offer' attached? Are these 'one-off', non-loyal, non-lifetime buyers worth the effort, or do they cost more than they are worth?

Sales promotions can be used to reward and retain loyal customers and acquire new customers if you have a good customer database. Ehrenberg suggests, 'Sales promotions need to be in the context of sustained advertising; otherwise trial will be once-only'. Sales promotions do not have to be one-off, short-term, tactical sales boosters. They can be more strategic – longer term, involving customer retention as well as acquisition and brand reinforcement – if they are planned carefully in advance and integrated with the other promotional tools.

Finally, even a great sales promotion fails if no one knows about it. Advertising, packaging, point-of-sale, publicity and sales force literature must support the sales promotion if it is to succeed. Regardless of dimensions all communications must integrate.

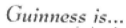

4-D tools – the 4th dimension: good sales promotions add value as well as reinforcing the brand values (Irishness and drink)

What is the difference between corporate image and corporate identity?

Corporate image has many dimensions. It is the aggregate of all the images and impressions perceived through all the senses including sight, sound, smell, touch and taste, as well as actual feelings experienced when dealing with an organization.

Images and impressions are created from a wide variety of sources beyond the normal communications tools. From buildings to behaviour of staff, from ethical policies to experiences of using a product or service... all of these create impressions and conjure up images of the organization.

You can see how integration must occur at many different levels throughout an organization. Corporate image is about perception. Corporate identity is about the tangible points of public contact – buildings, vehicles, uniforms – and the visual means of identifying an organization – names, logos and letterheads.

Corporate identity is projected through all the points of public contact. These include annual reports, exhibitions, advertisements, press launches, products and packaging, sales literature, interior and exterior designs of buildings, uniforms, van livery and signage, letterheads and, of course, the logo or signature of the business. The identity is a strategic asset. Like other assets it needs to be maintained and upgraded regularly. A good corporate identity helps sales by maintaining a clear profile, thus ensuring high awareness, which in turn is linked with sales. Many customers won't buy from a company they don't know. In addition, a well-managed corporate identity unconsciously gives customers a reassuring sense of order, and that adds credibility to all the communications of the business.

Coming back to corporate image – it can be good or bad, deliberate or unintentional. It should be planned and controlled. When choosing among similar products or services, many customers buy into the company behind the product – the corporate values. A good image adds credibility and value to all of the brands under the corporate umbrella. This also helps future launches of new products.

And a good image also helps staff morale and staff recruitment, strengthens financial relations and helps during a crisis as an organization with a good image enjoys a presumption of innocence.

Corporate image is often the responsibility of corporate communications and/or public relations. PR is probably best known for media relations – publicity, news conferences and press releases – all of which raise visibility. But much of PR's work occurs at an earlier stage – building credibility by winning third-party endorsements, ensuring smooth customer relations and developing sensible ethical policies.

This requires both functional, or horizontal, integration of communications. Corporate image is the result of everything an organization does – arguably, it is the ultimate integrator.

Corporate identity, like any other asset, needs to be maintained
and updated as the market moves on

How does the Internet integrate?

Multimedia combines many different media, such as television, radio, newspapers, books, magazines, photographs, drawings and text, linked together in an interactive way. It has got unknown potential and many dimensions or what is referred to as M-D.

Multimedia comes into your home or office, PC or TV using compact discs (CD ROMs/DVDs) or on-line with the Internet.

The Internet is just an international network of computers linked together. Once you're hooked up and plugged in you can rocket around computers across the world, drop into discussion groups, read bulletin boards, share ideas, photos, videos, articles, news and games. Visit virtual shopping malls, buy products, tour Universal Studios, the Louvre in Paris or watch the Rolling Stones play a concert.

The Internet can integrate with: sales by providing somewhere to offer advice, information and even sell; PR by spreading news, managing a crisis and lobbying regulatory bodies; advertising by offering a new medium to show ads; research by giving access to areas of interest – whether life-threatening diseases, world poverty, markets, new trends or new products.

The Internet is also used for internal communications among staff nationally and internationally – sharing expertise and information, preparing presentations, pitches and simply meeting colleagues around the world.

The Internet also helps customer service. Some companies save millions of dollars by putting multimedia service packages on to the Net so that customers can service themselves.

Estimates suggest that hundreds of millions of customers will be moving out of the marketplace and into market space – cyber-space – the new electronic frontier. Many marketers are setting up web sites – electronic trading posts. Despite the rush to colonize cyber-space, this vast frontier has many isolated sites. Travellers zip around unseen on a web of electronic back roads. Marketers need to erect signposts along the back roads of cyber-space to help to guide the fast-moving customer to their trading post or home page. Once there, travellers don't wait without reward. Items of interest have to pull the customer further into electronic rooms. Amidst a sea of multi-mediocrity, the sophisticated traveller moves on – never to return if disappointed by the first visit.

Web sites need sufficient investment, and should be integrated into the rest of the communications mix. They need to be interesting, carefully designed, updated and responded to if a dialogue is to be generated with customers: a conversation between the brand itself and the buyer – on a global scale – the marketer's dream.

The Internet is a new communications tool – a discrete form of promotion, but definitely not for direct mail. This non-linear, interactive tool can engage customers. It is a way of extending, enhancing and strengthening the brand values in both an interactive and truly integrated way.

Items of interest have to pull the customer further into electronic rooms. Cyber travellers don't wait without reward. Amidst a sea of multi-mediocrity, the sophisticated traveller moves on – never to return if disappointed by the first visit

What are IMC's 10 golden rules?

Despite the many benefits of Integrated Marketing Communications (or IMC), there are also many barriers. Here's how you can ensure you become integrated and stay integrated… 10 golden rules of integration.

1. Get senior management support for the initiative by ensuring they understand the benefits of IMC.

2. Integrate at different levels of management. Put 'integration' on the agenda for various types of management meetings – whether annual reviews or creative sessions. Horizontally – ensure that all managers, not just marketing managers, understand the importance of a consistent message – whether on delivery trucks or product quality. Also ensure that advertising, PR and sales promotions staff are integrating their messages. To do this, you must have carefully planned internal communications, that is, good internal marketing.

3. Ensure the design manual or even a brand book is used to maintain common visual standards for the use of logos, typefaces, colours, and so on.

4. Focus on a clear marketing communications strategy. Have crystal-clear communications objectives, clear positioning statements, and link core values into every communication. Ensure all communications add value to (instead of dilute) the brand or organization. Exploit areas of sustainable competitive advantage.

5. Start with a zero budget. Start from scratch. Build a new communications plan. Specify what you need to do so as to achieve your objectives. In reality, the budget you get is often less than you ideally need, so you may have to prioritize communications activities accordingly.

6. Think customers first. Wrap communications around the customers' buying process. Identify the stages they go through before, during and after a purchase. Select communication tools that are right for each stage. Develop a sequence of communications activities that help the customer to move easily through each stage.

7. Build relationships and brand values. All communications should help to develop stronger relationships with customers. Ask how each communication tool helps to do this. Remember, customer retention is as important as customer acquisition.

8. Develop a good marketing information system that defines who needs what information when. A customer database, for example, can help the telesales, direct marketing and sales force. IMC can help to define, collect and share vital information.

9. Share artwork and other media. Consider how, say, advertising imagery can be used in mail shots, exhibition stands, Christmas cards, news releases and web sites.

10. Be prepared to change it all. Learn from experience. Constantly search for the optimum communications mix. Test. Test. Test. Improve each year. 'Kaizen'.

Just a few ways to beat the barriers and enjoy the benefits of integrated marketing communications.

Get IMC onto the agenda

Notes

[1]Check out the Hall of Fame in Marketing CD ROM Title 10: Integrated Marketing Communications (Multimedia Marketing Consortium, London) later for more about missions.

[2]Professor Peter Doyle on Relationship Marketing, Marketing CD ROM Title 10: Integrated Marketing Communications, Multimedia Marketing Consortium, London.

[3]You can see more on databases in the video browser later in Marketing CD ROM Title 10: Integrated Marketing Communications, Multimedia Marketing Consortium, London.

[4]Professor Peter Doyle Marketing CD ROM Title 10: Integrated Marketing Communications, Multimedia Marketing Consortium, London.

glossary

A

Above the line   Advertising is considered to be above the line. Traditionally, advertising agencies charged commission on advertising which was 'above the line'. Other work by the agency such as design of sales promotions, mail shots and PR activities were charged a fixed fee and appeared on the agency bill as 'below the line'.

Advertising   Use of 'paid for space' in a publication, for instance, time on television, radio or cinema, usually as a means of persuading people to take a particular course of action, or to reach a point of view. May also be taken to include posters or other outdoor advertising – (see also 'above the line' advertising and 'below the line' advertising).

Advertising campaign   A planned sequence of advertisements.

Agents   Represent an organization and sell on their behalf. Usually paid by a percentage commission on sales. Unlike distributors, agents do not hold or buy stock. They just make contacts, take / win orders and pass the order on to the producer who subsequently delivers the goods.

AIDA   A model which maps some of the mental stages through which a customer passes en route purchasing a product or service: awareness, interest, desire and action.

Ansoff Matrix   A matrix that categorizes growth opportunities between existing products in existing markets, existing products in new markets, new products in existing markets and new products in new markets. Igor Ansoff created four classic growth options: market penetration through increased market share – marketing existing products into existing markets; market development through marketing existing products into new markets; product development through creating and launching new products into existing markets; and diversification, the riskiest option of all, launching new products into new markets.

Armchair shopping   Customers buy from inside their own home or office and delivery follows suit – directly into the home or the office. This is 'armchair shopping' since customers do not have to get up, go out, shop and traipse wearily home again. Includes direct mail, door-to-door selling, telesales, network retailing, television shopping channels and, of course, the Internet.

Attitude   A learnt predisposition to respond in a consistently favourable or unfavourable manner with respect to a given object. Such attitudes are a result of experiences, awareness + wants + needs of individuals. Since an understanding of attitudes helps to understand behaviour, marketers need to be acquainted with the subject so as to make informed assumptions about future consumer behaviour.

Augmented product   On top of this tangible product are more intangibles which augment, or increase the value of the product. Called the 'augmented product', this can include guarantees and services like credit facilities, delivery, installation, training, advice, servicing, insurance, and more.

B

Behaviour The actions of an individual or group in a given situation.

'Below the line' 'Below the line' advertising is considered to be 'above the line'. Traditionally, advertising agencies charged commission on advertising which was 'above the line'. Other work by the agency such as design of sales promotions, mail shots and PR activities were charged a fixed fee and appeared on the agency bill as 'below the line'.

Boston matrix Boston matrix can help to analyse the product portfolio. Senior managers need to know which products generate surplus cash, which ones need extra marketing budgets to support them and which ones should be deleted. They also need to know if they can fund the development of new products. Products in growth markets generally require cash to help them grow as cash gets tied up in working capital (stocks and debtors). Products that enjoy relatively large market shares in low-growth 'mature markets' are the 'cash cows' that generate the surplus cash which in turn funds other products, such as the high-growth 'star' products. 'Stars' soak up working capital funds, but they may become tomorrow's cash cows.

Bottom-up planning Plans created by lower levels of management or staff without input from higher levels of management.

Bottom-up sales forecasting Each sales person makes their own forecast for their own product or service in their particular area. These are then all added together to get a bottom-up forecast.

Brand manager Marketing manager responsible for a single brand.

Break even Break even is the point where no losses and no profits are made. The point where losses stop and profits start. The minimum number of units required to be sold to avoid losing money. BEP (break-even point) is calculated by dividing unit contribution (C) into total fixed costs (FC): $BEP = FC/C$.

Budget Resources required for marketing activities – usually money.

C

Cash flow The movement of cash coming in through sales and other revenues and cash going out to pay for expenditures.

Channel conflict Different distribution channel members (eg manufacturers, wholesalers, retailers) sometimes fight for the same customer, market control and most of the channel profit. Conflict can occur when a firm uses multiple distribution channels by dealing directly with customers as well as going through intermediaries like distributors.

Closing a sale When the customer agrees to buy and undertakes to pay (eg signs an order form). Arguably, it is the most difficult part of selling.

Communications mix Sometimes called 'the promotions mix' or 'the marketing communications mix', it includes advertising, sales promotion, PR and direct marketing. The promotions mix is one of the 4Ps of the marketing mix.

Competitor analysis Involves analysing your competitors, their strengths and weaknesses, and their likely strategic moves.

Conjoint analysis Measures the individual as well as joint effects of a set of variables (Bradley); helps to identify the best combination of, say, product benefits to present to a target market. Conjoint analysis allows different combinations of prices, features, benefits and brand names to be evaluated so that the marketers can identify the best marketing mix for any particular segment.

Consumer The end user of a product or service. Not always the buyer.

Contingency plans Alternative plans prepared in case things do not go according to the main marketing plan.

Contribution The difference between selling price and variable cost. This amount 'contributes' towards the repayment of the fixed overheads. Break-even point can be calculated by dividing the unit contribution into the fixed overhead costs to find exactly how many units need to be sold to avoid losses and break even.

Core product There is usually a core (reason) or benefit at the heart of every product purchase which ultimately satisfies an aroused need. This is intangible (you cannot touch it or feel it) and is referred to as the core product. Driving a particular car may make you feel good, powerful, successful, or maybe it just takes you to work.

Corporate identity Corporate identity is the visual means of identifying an organization. Logos and names are only a part of the identity, albeit important parts. Corporate identity is projected through all the points of public contact, ie all the communications mix and more. This includes sales literature, advertisements, press launches, exhibitions, annual reports, products and packaging, interior and exterior design of buildings, uniforms, livery and signage, letterheads and, of course, the logo. The identity is a strategic asset. Like other assets it needs to be maintained and upgraded.

Corporate strategy Setting down of long-term plans of development in a methodical manner, based upon all the available facts, and relating them to the ultimate goals of a company and the ways it intends to achieve them. Timescales vary from three to 10 years (even more in certain industries). Fundamental to the preparation of a corporate plan is the need to define exactly the area of business in which to be operative. A second requirement is that any such plan must be flexible, subject to regular updating, as events move to change the criteria upon which it is based.

Correlation A statistical relationship between variables such as sales of ice cream and the weather.

Cost plus
A common method of setting price is to estimate the costs of a product and to add a percentage to achieve a certain margin of profit. This is known as cost-plus pricing, and there are several problems with it. Most companies don't actually know what their real costs are product by product. As the volume of production, distribution and selling activity increases, costs change. Even then, what percentage should be added to set a price? 10 per cent? 20 per cent? 50 per cent?

Creative process
The cognitive process of generating ideas, usually for promotional purposes.

Credence qualities
Credence values are those values that are hard to evaluate even after the service. Even with experience, performance may still be difficult to measure. How do you know if your car service, facelift, or rewiring is of high quality? These are 'credence qualities' – features that are hard to evaluate even after the event. These often abstract variables make buying services more risky.

D

Deadlines
Schedules and delivery dates/times.

Decision-making unit
All those individuals or groups who have an influence upon buying a product or service.

Demographic
Population statistics such as age, sex, social-class, etc. Used in segmentation.

Demographics
The statistical analysis (or division) of a population/audience/market by several variables which include age, sex, social status.

Desk research
Checks secondary sources before carrying out the more expensive primary research.

Differential advantages
An advantage which (a) customers perceive and want, and (b) the competition does not have.

Direct-marketing Direct marketing gives an organization access to a target market directly. Direct-response advertising, direct mail, door-to-door selling, telesales, network retailing, television shopping channels and, of course, the Internet are all direct-marketing tools.

Direct-response advertising Advertising which asks the audience to respond directly and immediately by means of filling in a coupon or calling a telephone number. Direct-response advertising solicits a physical response. This is different to other advertising which creates a platform of awareness and emotional feelings.

Distribution penetration Penetrating the distribution network to a certain level to ensure its availability to customers.

Durables Consumer products can be categorized by perishability or durability. Consumer durables, like TVs and fridges, are very different from non-durables like soft drinks and detergents – FMCGs – fast moving consumer goods.

E

Elasticity Price elasticity, or price sensitivity, suggests the sales changes in unit sales affected by changes in price.

Emotional–rational dichotomy The reasons for buying are sometimes split between emotional reasons and rational reasons.

Exclusive distribution Exclusive distribution can have two different meanings: (1) When intermediaries like agents or distributors want to be the only distributors, the sole distributors, or have the 'exclusive distribution rights' to sell a product or service within a certain area. (2) Restricted distribution – to upmarket exclusive retail outlets as in the case of certain fashion clothes.

Exhibitions A display of goods by one or more organizations to potential customers. A form of sales promotion, eg, the motor show at Birmingham NEC.

Experience curve	As the organization produces more, it becomes more efficient. Better sourcing of materials, new production processes, labour efficiencies, economies of scale and improved product designs all reduce costs. More customers with more loyalty mean less promotion costs.
Experience qualities	Buyers with experience draw upon experience qualities – previous experiences of the service in terms of say, speed, friendliness, performance, etc.
Exploratory research	Searches for the issues which sometimes need to be included in a bigger quantitative survey.
Extensive problem-solving process	Searching, collecting and careful evaluation of information about a product or service before deciding on which brand to buy. *See* High involvement.

F

Field marketing	Field sales force is an organization's sales force. Some organizations hire contract sales forces from a 'field marketing' agency. These agencies supply a temporary sales team for a fixed period of time, typically during seasonal peaks and during special promotions.
First to market	Developing and launching a new product before the competition launch their version.
Fixed costs	Fixed costs are costs which basically remain fixed, in the short term at least, regardless of how many units are produced and sold. They include rent and rates, management salaries, and so on. These are also called fixed overheads costs, say £10,000.
Floating target	A target market whose profile remains constant but whose members change over time as they drift in and out of the buying window.

G

Geodemo-graphics	Mix geographic and demographic data together to find clusters of demographic groups within certain geographical areas.
Global competition	Global competition refers to all forms of competition on a worldwide scale.
Global marketing	A marketing campaign that is aimed at markets all over the world.
Group product managers	Marketing managers responsible for a group of products and brands.

H

Hall tests	Respondents are invited into a hall or room where research is then carried out on the new products, packs advertisements that are on show.
Heterogeneous	Heterogeneity, or variability, means that not everything or everyone is the same. In services heterogeneity makes every service delivered at least a little bit different. This makes it difficult to standardize the quality of services.
High-contact activities	Most services have a mixture of high- and low-contact with customers. For example, the bulk of dry cleaning services are done without the customer being present (maybe in a back room), while acupuncture services are performed in the presence of the customer. The invoicing (low-contact activity) and appointment-making may be done again in a back room without the customer's presence.
High involvement	High-involvement purchases are expensive, high-risk, infrequently bought products or services. Here the buyer goes through an extensive problem-solving process.

Horizontal marketing systems	Horizontal marketing systems allow/encourage different organizations to share their expertise and give each other access to new customer segments.

I

IMC – integrated marketing communications	All communications and messages are carefully linked together to produce a coherent, distinctive, harmonic image which differentiates the product/brand against the competition. It brings together all forms of communications within an organization into a single 'seamless solution'. Unintegrated or disintegrated communications send disjointed messages, dilute impact and sometimes confuse, frustrate and arguably arouse anxiety in customers. Integrated communications present a reassuring sense of order.
In-depth interviews	A qualitative research method which involves discussions on a one-to-one basis.
Information audit	Specifies who needs what information when. The audit can also list sources of information.
In-house teams	Staff from within the organization as opposed to an outside agency, eg, in-house public relations team as opposed to using an outside PR agency. In reality, they are sometimes mixed together, ie the in-house team may be supplemented by an outside agency and its resources.
Integrated approach	A management style which seeks to take account of marketing (or something else) in all decisions. Thereby marketing thinking is integrated (part of) all decision making.
Integrated communications	With careful planning, communications tools such as advertising, direct mail, sales promotions, point-of-sale, etc can be integrated so that the message is consistent, overall impact is increased and costs reduced. *See* IMC – integrated marketing communications.

Intensive distribution	Wide availability; deep distribution penetration; mass distribution into all outlets, eg, confectionery tends to be widely available.
Intermediaries	Organizations or individuals in the distribution channel, eg wholesalers and retailers.
Internal marketing	Promoting a marketing orientation to all internal staff. Designing and implementing appropriate activities to ensure constant improvement and motivation of all internal staff.

J

JIT	Just-in-time delivery is a system that delivers exact quantities only when they are required and ready to be used immediately.

K

Kaizen	The Japanese refer to continuous year-to-year improvement as 'kaizen'.

L

Leads	Possible customers; prospective customers; prospects; enquirers; enquiries or leads generated from mail shots, advertisements and exhibitions. The quality of the lead should be checked so that the best leads, called 'hot prospects', or hot leads, get special attention.
Learnings	Marketers constantly seek to learn from their experience and to improve their performances. Some companies formalise this process and incorporate the key things a marketing manager learns into their next set of plans.
Lifestyle	The way in which someone or a group of people live their lives.

Lifetime customers	Customers who repeatedly buy the same brand throughout their buying life.
Lifetime value	The total amount spent by one customer on a product or service during his/her lifetime.
Limited problem-solving process	A situation where the buyer has some experience of buying a particular product or service. *See* Extensive problem-solving process.
Line extension	*See* Product line.
Liquidation	When a company becomes insolvent it goes bust! Its assets are liquidated or sold off for cash. Bankrupt.
List explosion	The proliferation of a vast array of different types of direct mail lists.
Loss leaders	Loss leaders are products or services offered at low prices (often below cost) to entice customers into buying other products or services.
Low-contact activities	Most services have a mixture of high- and low-contact with customers. For example, the bulk of dry cleaning services are done without the customer being present (maybe in a back room), while acupuncture services are performed in the presence of the customer. The invoicing (low-contact activity) and appointment-making may be done again in a back room without the customer's presence.
Low involvement	Low-involvement purchases are frequently bought, such as low-value purchases like a can of beans. There is little risk and hence the buyer spends less time and effort making the decision. *See* High involvement.

M

3Ms	Three key resources: men, money and minutes. Men means men and women, money mean budgets and minutes mean time.

Macro factors	Those factors affecting an organization that are beyond the control of that organization, but which the organization must take account of.
Mailshot	Sending letters to a target audience – eg distribution of information to potential customers via the post with the purpose of increasing sales and profit.
Marginal cost	Marginal cost is the extra cost of making one extra unit. It is, for example, the difference in total costs when you produce 101 units instead of 100.
Marginal pricing	Marginal pricing looks at sales forecasts and sets a price based on the lower marginal costs that can be achieved in the future. This enables you to set prices below competitors.
Market fragmentation	A term used to describe a market that has many different clearly identifying segments.
Market reports	Provides information on markets, their size, structure, key players, their market share, trends, prices, and more. These reports are published annually and are available as secondary sources.
Mass markets	Markets which include a very large number of potential and actual customers – eg the fast-moving consumer goods market.
Me-too product	A similar type of product.
Micro factors	The elements of the environment within which an organization operates where it has a significant degree of control, eg its products or services, its staff.
Mind-share	The share of a distributor's mind that your product or service gets. Winning the battle for the distributor's share of mind can be more important than many other marketing strategies. It requires the maintenance of high levels of motivation among distributors so that they are interested in and motivated by your products or services.

MIS	A marketing information system should provide all the information for effective marketing decisions. This will vary from market research to reading the paper, but it must be recorded and be available.
Mission statement	This is a conconcisely written statement which embraces the organizations goals and values, while defining which business the organization is in.
Ms-resources	What a manager needs to do his/her job. Marketing plans must contain at least three resources – the 3Ms: men, money and minutes. Men means men and women, money means budgets and minutes means time.
Multi-channel network	Basically mixes different distribution channels together – some direct and others indirect. This can involve the supplier's own sales force as well as a network of intermediaries and their sales forces.
Multi-channel systems	Basically mixes different distribution channels together using both direct and indirect channels. This can involve the supplier's own sales force as well as a net-work of intermediaries and their sales forces. *See* Channel conflict.
Multi-level marketing	Network retailing; network marketing; multi-level marketing. This is where sales people recruit other salespeople so that they sell for them, and so on.
Multinational	An organization which operates in several countries.
Multiple channels	Selling and distributing to customers directly, as well as distributing through vending machines, indepen-dent retailers and mainstream retail chains. *See* Channel conflict.
Mutual benefit	The outcome of an action whereby all parties involved are subsequently better off.
Mystery shoppers	Customer service can be measured by fake customers (mystery shoppers) who report directly back to the organization.

N

Near environment	The near environment is closer to the organization than the far environment (*see* Step 1). Although external to the organization, the near environment is close to the organization and it includes Step 2 variables: structure of the industry, trends in the marketplace, micro-economic and power forces shaping the industry.
Niche marketing	Marketing to a small/specialist market segment.

O

Objective	Objectives are the quantified goals that state 'where you want to go'.
On-pack offers	A sales promotion on a pack.
Order getter	A sales representative who likes to go after and 'get' new business. An 'order taker', on the other hand, is a sales representative who likes to service existing customers.
Order taker	A sales representative who likes to service existing customers. An 'order getter', on the other hand, is a sales representative who likes to go after and 'get' new business.
Organic growth	Growth in sales generated by an organization from within as opposed to growth in sales created by acquiring other external organization's and their sales.
Organizational objectives	These are the goals of the organization.
OTS	Opportunities to see is one way of measuring the size of the audience. The number of exposures or opportunities which a particular audience has to see a specific ad. An audience of seven million viewers delivers seven million OTSs.

P

Packaging The pack must protect, communicate and provide convenience to user, distributor and retailer.

Pan-European marketing A marketing campaign that is aimed at the whole of Europe.

Patent A patent legally protects a product against being duplicated by anyone other than the patent holder for a fixed time period.

POS Point-of-sale (also known in the US as point of purchase); whether it is a tailored display rack, dump bin, bobble card, bottle collar or something more inventive, point-of-sale materials offer a last chance to grab a customer. Who knows what goes through a customer's mind during the last 30 seconds before a purchase? We do know it can be influenced by a clever piece of POS.

Positioning The choice of mix which conveys the image and value of a product or brand in the mind of its target audience.

Price The amount of money which is required in exchange for a product/service.

Proactive An approach which seeks to anticipate events and plan accordingly.

Product Anything capable of satisfying a want, need or desire.

Product launch The release of a new product or service into the marketplace is usually supported by a range of promotional activities.

Product life cycle Course of a product's life in terms of sales and profitability from its development to its decline.

Product line A product line is a string of products grouped together for marketing or technical reasons. For example, Guinness started as a single-product company. Since then it has extended the product line to fill market needs as they have emerged.

Promotion	Any device designed to increase consumer purchases, eg free samples, off-price labels, banded offers, premium offers, competitions and personality promotions.
Promotional programme	The plan for all promotional activity over a certain time period. Including objectives, costs, revenues, promotional tools, evaluation, etc.
Psychographic	A science of population statistics relating to psychological variables such as attitudes, beliefs, opinions, etc. Used in segmentation.
Publicity	Unpaid media coverage.
Public relations	The planned and sustained effort to establish and maintain goodwill and mutual understanding between an organization and its public.

R

Reactive	A management style/approach whereby events happen and then management acts to compensate for these events.
Regression analysis	A mathematical technique which finds a statistical relationship between variables such as sales of ice cream and the weather.
Relationship marketing	The development of good relationships and repeat purchases with customers over the long term.
Resources	What a manager needs to do his/her job. Marketing plans must contain at least three resources – 3Ms: men, money and minutes.
Retail audits	Measure market sales, competitor's sales, market share, prices, special offers, stock levels week by week or day by day.
Return on investment	Return means profit. Profit on investment identifies how profitable any particular investment is.

Routinized response behaviour	Whenever a need is stimulated, a particular brand is automatically purchased.

S

Sales force	The team of sales people.
Saturated markets	A market is saturated if there is no potential for profit growth as consumer needs are adequately met.
Search qualities	Tangible clues that can be evaluated before purchase. Services are low in 'search' qualities. You cannot pick them up and inspect their quality before purchase.
Secondary research	Uses research already carried out by someone else for some other purpose.
Selective distribution	Carefully chosen distributors/retailers, eg speciality goods as in the case of car repair kits.
SMART	Objectives should be Specific, Measurable, Achievable, Realistic and Time-related.
SOSTAC	An acronym which helps the planning process: Situation analysis, Objectives, Strategy, Tactics, Action and Control.
SOSTAC + 3Ms	An acronym which helps the planning process: Situation analysis, Objectives, Strategy, Tactics, Action and Control + 3Ms. The last are three key resources which every plan must have = men*, money and minutes (*men means men and women), devised by P R Smith, author, *Marketing Communications – An Integrated Approach* (1993), Kogan Page, London.
Step 1	The uncontrollable variables in the 'far' environment, which include social, technical, economic and political developments.

Step 2	Variables which include the structure of the industry, trends in the marketplace, micro-economic and power forces shaping the industry.
Strategy	Strategy explains how objectives will be achieved and gives direction to all the subsequent tactical activities. Strategy summarises all the tactics. *See* Corporate strategy.
Synergy	2 + 2 = 5.

T

Tangible product	Beyond the intangible or non-physical core benefit, products have a tangible dimension. These are the physical aspects of the product: its features, quality level, design, packaging, etc. This is the actual tangible product (the part of the product you can touch and feel).
Targeting	The selecting of market segments for which a product or service will be designed and marketed.
Target market	A market segment selected, or targeted, for sales.
Telesales	A team of sales people who operate by phone only. Sometimes their job is only to make appointments for other sales people. Other times the telesales team will be involved in directly selling a product, service or concept.
Time management	A system of managing this limited resource, time.
Top-down sales forecasting	As opposed to bottom-up forecasting, top-down does not draw on the sales force's individual forecasts but uses other forecasting systems, some of which are sophisticated computer models.
Trade-off	A compromise.

Transactional marketing	Short-term approach to making a single sale as opposed to developing longer-term relationships and winning repeat business. *See* Relationship marketing.

U

Upmarket	The wealthier section of the market: higher income customers; prestige products / services.
Usage	Describes the frequency of use and also the way a product or service is used, ie the benefits it delivers.
USP	Unique selling proposition – something unique about a product / service and / or its brand image which might help it to sell.

V

Variable costs	Variable costs are costs which vary directly with the number of units produced – they can include raw materials and labour.
VAT	Value added tax.

W

Word association	A projective technique which throws the respondent's ego off-guard and allow the inner, deeper feelings to be expressed (a qualitative research tool).
Word of mouth	Refers to a situation where one party learns about a product or service second hand from another party who has knowledge of it. Word of mouth is a powerful persuader. Customers talk to each other. Dissatisfied customers tell at least two or three times more people than satisfied customers. You can see why service companies try to get their customers to tell them first about any problems or complaints.

Z

Zero risk No risk – a decision or choice where the outcome is known with certainty.

index

THE MULTIMEDIA MARKETING CONSORTIUM PRESENTS

THE MARKETING CD ROMS

a series of ten world class CD ROMs
covering a complete course on marketing

Enter the world of multimedia. Improve your organization's marketing skills and save money simultaneously. Watch world gurus and top marketing managers reveal their secrets of success. Enjoy a whole new experience.

Why use The Marketing CD ROMs?

- Improve your organization's marketing skills
- Create a new awareness of marketing throughout the organization
- Reduce mistakes by copying how the experts do it first time
- Reduce training costs by saving time and money tied up in travel and accommodation
- Reduce costs even further by sharing the CD ROMs around
- Broaden the access to marketing training – let everyone come on board
- Reward staff with state of the art training materials
- Learn the right marketing jargon

How does it work?

Choose an area of interest. Listen to the expert and enjoy the slide show. Explore additional examples in the hyperlinks. Assess yourself with Questions and Answers. Visit the Hall of Fame where Theodore Levitt, Rosabeth Moss Kanter, Kenichi Ohmae, Philip Kotler and Peter Doyle reveal the secrets of marketing success. Watch them, convert them to text, add your own notes. Mix your thoughts and theirs. Use the video browsers to see marketing managers, from Coca–Cola to Concorde and Microsoft to Manchester United, explain how they market their products and services successfully. Use in a group, in a department meeting or on your own, at work, at home or while travelling.

THE TEN MARKETING CD ROMS

1. History, Definition and Concept of Marketing
2. Segmentation, Positioning and the Marketing Mix
3. Marketing Planning
4. Buyer Behaviour
5. Marketing Research
6. Product Decisions
7. Service Decisions
8. Pricing Decisions
9. Distribution Decisions
10. Integrated Marketing Communications

EACH MARKETING CD ROM CONTAINS:

- Tutorials – up to 12 tutorials combining video with graphics
- Self Assessment – 100+ Questions & Answers
- Hall of Fame – World Wide Gurus reveal the secrets of success
- Picture Browser – over 100 images
- Video Browser – additional video clips of top marketers in action
- Glossary – over 200 pieces of jargon defined
- Text-tools – convert video into text
- Notepad – mix your own electronic notes with the gurus' text
- Summary – progress check and key point summary
- Hyperlinks – related examples and linked materials
- Save – your progress, scores, notes taken and hyperlinks explored

'...**exciting new material**...' The Chartered Institute of Marketing

'...**instantaneous access to the best marketing minds in the world**...' The Marketing Council

'...**a valuable resource to industry**...' The Institute of Practitioners in Advertising

For more information visit the Web site below or contact Paul Smith directly at:
The Multimedia Marketing Consortium
London Guildhall University
84 Moorgate
London EC2M 6SQ
Telephone: (0171) 320 1454
Fax: (0171) 320 1465
E-mail: psmith@lgu.ac.uk
Web: www.lgu.ac.uk/lgu/mmm

Also by P R Smith

Marketing Communications (second edition)
An Integrated Approach

First published in 1993, *Marketing Communications* is firmly established as an international bestseller: P R Smith's contribution to the acceptance and understanding of an integrated approach to marketing communications is now universally recognized. Marketing professionals and students alike have benefited from his pragmatic and original approach. Indeed, it is the recommended reading text for the Chartered Institute of Marketing's Promotional Practice module and included on the Marketing Society's prestigious list of marketing classics.

This latest edition has been thoroughly updated and revised: new short cases, up-to-date statistics, fresh illustrations and photographs, along with a more pan-European flavour, all combine to bring it right up-to-date with the current international business scene. Several chapters have been completely rewritten, and the larger format and redesigned text layout will make it easier for reading and studying.

Three major features of this new second edition are:

- Golden rules of IMC (Integrated Marketing Communications) – a new section which covers the benefits, the barriers and the golden rules.
- SOSTAC Planning System – a unique system, tested on hundreds of marketing managers, which provides a simple and structured approach to planning.
- The Internet – a major new chapter giving an in-depth look at the benefits and barriers and how to integrate the Internet into an overall marketing communications strategy.

The prime aim of *Marketing Communications* is to provide readers with a comprehensive framework to better understand the individual elements of the marketing communications mix and their collective effectiveness.

Continuing in the same lively style as before, the new edition is packed with visuals, practical tips and useful insights. The cases and examples are drawn from a diverse range of organizations and show successful solutions in action.

Kogan Page
120 Pentonville Road
London N1 9JN
Tel: 0171 278 0433
Fax: 0171 837 6348
E-mail: kpinfo@kogan-page.co.uk

Also by Paul Smith with Chris Berry and Alan Pulford

Strategic Marketing Communications
New Ways to Build and Integrate Communications

Imagine this...
You have a marketing strategy, and advertising strategy, and, if you're organized, a sales promotion strategy, a direct mail strategy and an exhibitions strategy... but you have no overall communication strategy which drives all of these communications tools in the same direction. *Strategic Marketing Communications* tackles this problem as an issue of growing importance for all marketing professionals. The subtitle, *New Ways to Build and Integrate Communications*, reflects the new ideas, new models, and new thinking blended together in this book.

Not an ordinary book...
This is not just an ordinary textbook: it is an interactive learning tool packed with practical examples, short cases, model documents and checklists to help you build communications plans and strategies simply and easily. A new planning system, called SOSTAC, brings it all together by showing you how to write the perfect plan within minutes. All in all, if you are faced with the task of creating a communications strategy, it will enable you to develop new ways of achieving competitive advantage.

After reading this book you will know...
- How to generate marketing communication strategies
- How to integrate all of the communications tools
- How to write better marketing communications plans
- How to exploit the Internet opportunity
- Much more about communications and how they can work more effectively

This book builds on, and is a sequel to, Paul Smith's best-selling *Marketing Communications – An Integrated Approach* (which covers all the communications tools individually).

The Chartered Institute of Marketing
This book has been specifically written to cover the CIM Diploma subject, Marketing Communications Strategy (while P R Smith's *Marketing Communications – An Integrated Approach* covers the CIM Advanced Certificate subject, Promotional Practice).

Kogan Page
120 Pentonville Road
London N1 9JN
Tel: 0171 278 0433
Fax: 0171 837 6348
E-mail: kpinfo@kogan-page.co.uk

Up to 5
Free Books
(until 30 June 2000)

When you order the Marketing CD ROMs (see information on pages 275–76)

Yes, [ ] (please tick) I want to order the following:

[ ] 1 x set of 10 Marketing CD ROMs @ £1,000 + VAT*
   plus 5 free books selected from book list on page 280

[ ] Free Book 1 _____
                (Author)   (Title)   (ISBN No)

[ ] Free Book 2 _____
                (Author)   (Title)   (ISBN No)

[ ] Free Book 3 _____
                (Author)   (Title)   (ISBN No)

[ ] Free Book 4 _____
                (Author)   (Title)   (ISBN No)

[ ] Free Book 5 _____
                (Author)   (Title)   (ISBN No)

or

[ ] 1 x Marketing CD ROM @ £150.00+VAT* selected from the CD ROM list on page 276

_____   _____
(CD Title No)   (Marketing CD ROM Title)
plus one free book selected from book list on page 280

[ ] Free Book   _____
                (Author)   (Title)   (ISBN No)

Please invoice me and deliver to (block letters please):

Name: _____

Address: _____

_____

Signature: _____   Date: _____

*Please note – these prices are for a single user licence only. Multiple user licence prices are available from:

The Multimedia Marketing Consortium
Manchester Metropolitan University, Minshull House, Chorlton St, Manchester M1 3EU
Tel: 00 44 (0) 161 247 6052   Fax: 00 44 (0) 161 247 6301
Web site: www.lgu.ac.uk/lgu/mmm
E-mail: a.pulford@mmu.ac.uk

Choose your free book/s from this selection:

Book Title	Author	Normal Retail Price	ISBN
1. The 21st Century Manager – future focused skills for the next millennium	Di Kamp	14.99	0 7494 2950 X
2. Persuading Aristotle – a masterclass in the timeless art of persuasion	Peter Thompson	14.99	0 7494 3011 7
3. 12 Ladders to World Class Performance	David Drennan	16.99	0 7494 3000 1
4. Shakespeare on Management – leadership lessons for managers	Paul Corrigan	16.99	0 7494 2845 7
5. Driving Change – how the best companies are preparing for the 21st century	Jerry Yoram Wind and Jeremy Main	11.99	0 7494 3017 6
6. The War Lords – measuring strategy and tactics for competitive advantage	Jorge Vasconcellos e Sá	16.99	0 7494 2824 4
7. Running Board Meetings – tips and techniques for getting the best from them	Patrick Dunne	19.95 (HB) 12.99 (PB)	0 7494 3015 X 0 7494 3014 1
8. In the Company of Heroes – release your entrepreneurial spirit	David Hall	14.99	0 7494 3060 5
9. Releasing Creativity – how leaders can develop creative potential in their teams	John Whatmore	16.99	0 7494 3010 9
10. Mining The Internet – information gathering and research on the Internet	Brian Clegg	9.99	0 7494 3025 7
11. Connected Intelligence – the arrival of the Web society	Derrick de Kerckhove	12.99	0 7494 2657 8
12. Doing Business on the Internet	Simon Collin	15.99	0 7494 2710 8
13. How To Be Better At Customer Care	Timothy R V Foster	8.99	0 7494 2945 3
14. Marketing Communications – an integrated approach	P R Smith	21.95	0 7494 2699 3
15. Strategic Marketing Communications – new ways to build and integrate communications	P R Smith Chris Berry Alan Pulford	19.95	0 7494 2918 6
16. 11 Steps to Brand Heaven – the ultimate guide to buying an advertising campaign	Leonard Weinreich	18.99	0 7494 2894 5
17. The New Strategic Selling – the unique sales system proven successful by the world's best companies	Stephen E Heiman and Diane Sanchez	16.99	0 7494 2833 3
18. Practical Marketing and PR for the Small Business	Moi Ali	16.99	0 7494 2686 1
19. Your Home Office – a practical guide to using technology successfully	Peter Chatterton	7.99	0 7494 2768 X
20. Instant Time Management – practical tips, short cuts, exercises; reorganize your life and work now	Brian Clegg	9.99	0 7494 2963 1